AF342197

GRAPHIC PHOTO DESIGN

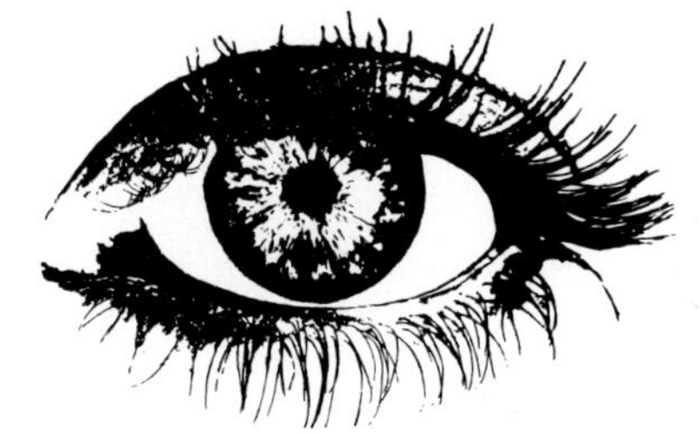

GRAPHIC PHOTO DESIGN

Lab Techniques in Color and Black & White

DIETER FRÖBISCH
HARTMUT LAMPRECHT

AMPHOTO
American Photographic Book Publishing Co., Inc.
Garden City, New York

Contents

Introduction 9

BLACK-AND-WHITE LAB TECHNIQUES
Paper Gradations 12
Continuous-Tone Enlargement, Negative 16
Continuous-Tone Enlargement, Unsharp 18
Motion 20
Multiple Exposures 22
Soft Contouring 24
Greased Glass Plate 26
Repetitive Copying, Positive 28
Repetitive Copying, Negative 30
Black-and-White Tonal Separation 32
Relief 34
Linear Relief 36
Pseudosolarization 38
Lines of Equal Density 42
Agfacontour Procedure 44
Screening 46
Screen Structures 50
Screen Structures 54
Three-Tone Screening 56
Screen Masks 58
Distortions 60
Superimposition 64

COLOR TONING

Toning   68
Albumin Glazing Dyes   70
Toning and Albumin Glazing Dyes   72
Felt-Tip Penning   74
Spray Technique   78
Colored Masks   80

COLOR-KEY

Color-Key   84
Tone Separation With Color-Key   90

COLOR LAB TECHNIQUES

Enlargement of Color Negative Film   94
False-Color Enlargements   96
Color-Slide Enlargements   98
Color-Tone Separation   100
Color Solarization   102
Color Solarization   104
Color Solarization   106
Agfacontour in Color   108
Color Relief   112
Color Relief   114

TYPOGRAPHY WITH PHOTOS

Typographic Modifications   118

Typographic Modifications   **120**
Typographic Modifications   **122**

GRAPHIC VARIATIONS
Photo-Graphics   **126**

PRINTING
Coarse-Color Screen   **132**
Fluorescent Colors   **134**
Fluorescent Colors   **136**
Metallic Colors   **138**
Hot Foil Stamping   **140**
Embossing   **142**

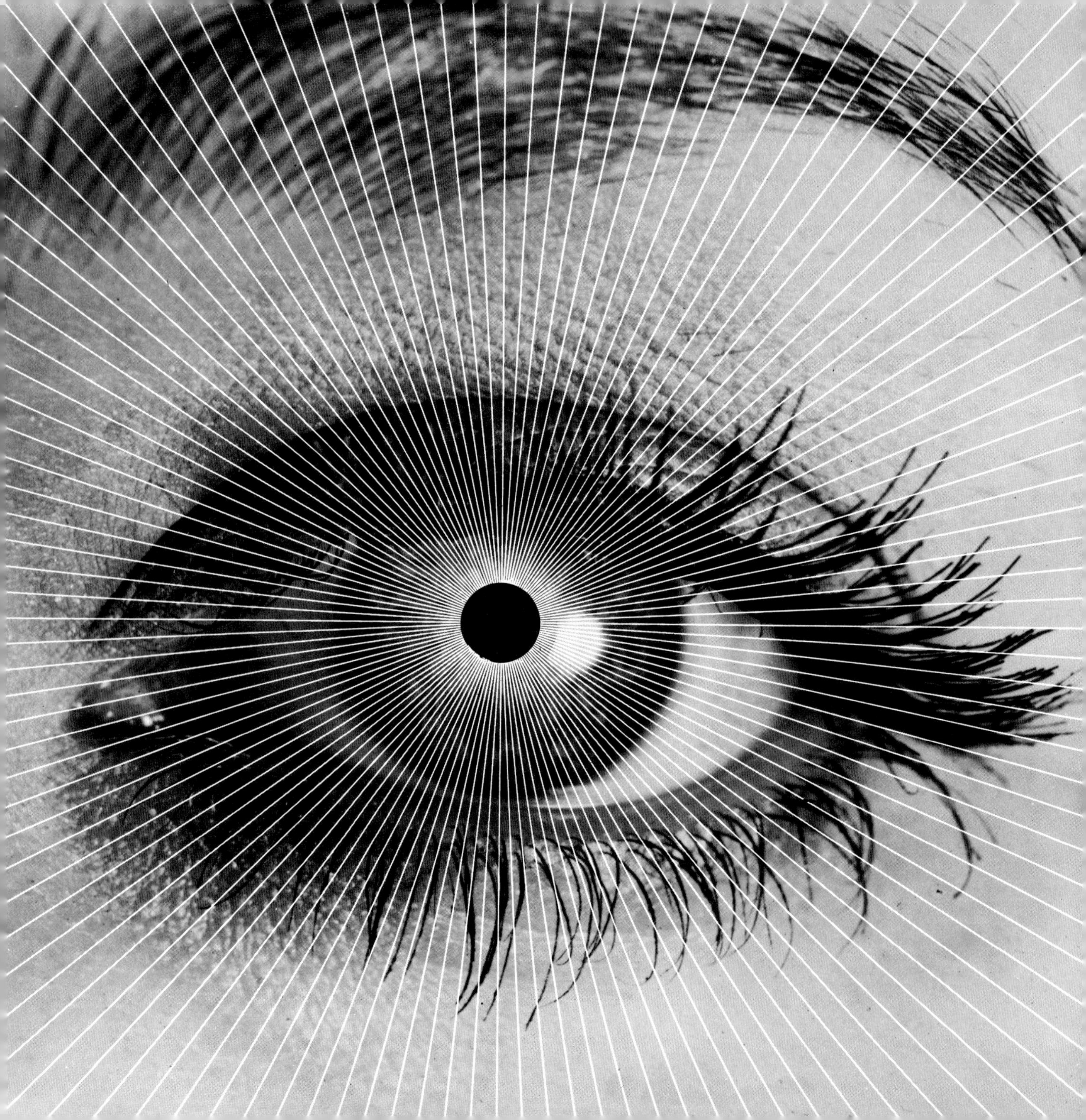

Introduction

How often does a great idea fail because of insufficient "know-how?" One relies upon well-known and dependable procedures and tries to keep away from experimenting.

Therefore, this book offers valuable help to any person who is already acquainted with the enlargement technique. The authors wish to present, in order, the many possibilities and to compare the most widely-used techniques.

To characterize differences, one has to show variations. For this reason, you will find many techniques shown on the same subject. The starting point for all the examples shown was a color transparency from which a black-and-white continuous-tone negative was taken. These selected procedures will become a vital help and reference for everyone who works with drafting and design.

We would like to thank Hochschule für Gestaltung Offenbach in Germany and the teachers Wilfried Indinger (Photography) and Wolfgang Sprang (Graphic Design) for all the help they gave us.

9

BLACK-AND-WHITE LAB TECHNIQUES

Paper Gradations

Procedure

(1) Position negative in enlarger.
(2) Determine image area and sharpness.
(3) Position photo paper.
(4) Find exposure time, and expose.
(5) Develop, stop, fix, wash, and dry.

To make enlargements which are of correct tonal values (caused by different negative contrasts), photographic paper of six different contrast grades is usually available. A negative with normal contrast will make a tone-correct copy on normal paper (No. 3). An intended deviation of this is achieved by using paper of extra-hard (No. 6) to extra-soft (No. 1) gradation.

Page 13: Enlargement on normal paper (No. 3)
Page 14: Enlargement on extra-hard paper (No. 6)
Page 15: Enlargement on extra-soft paper (No. 1)

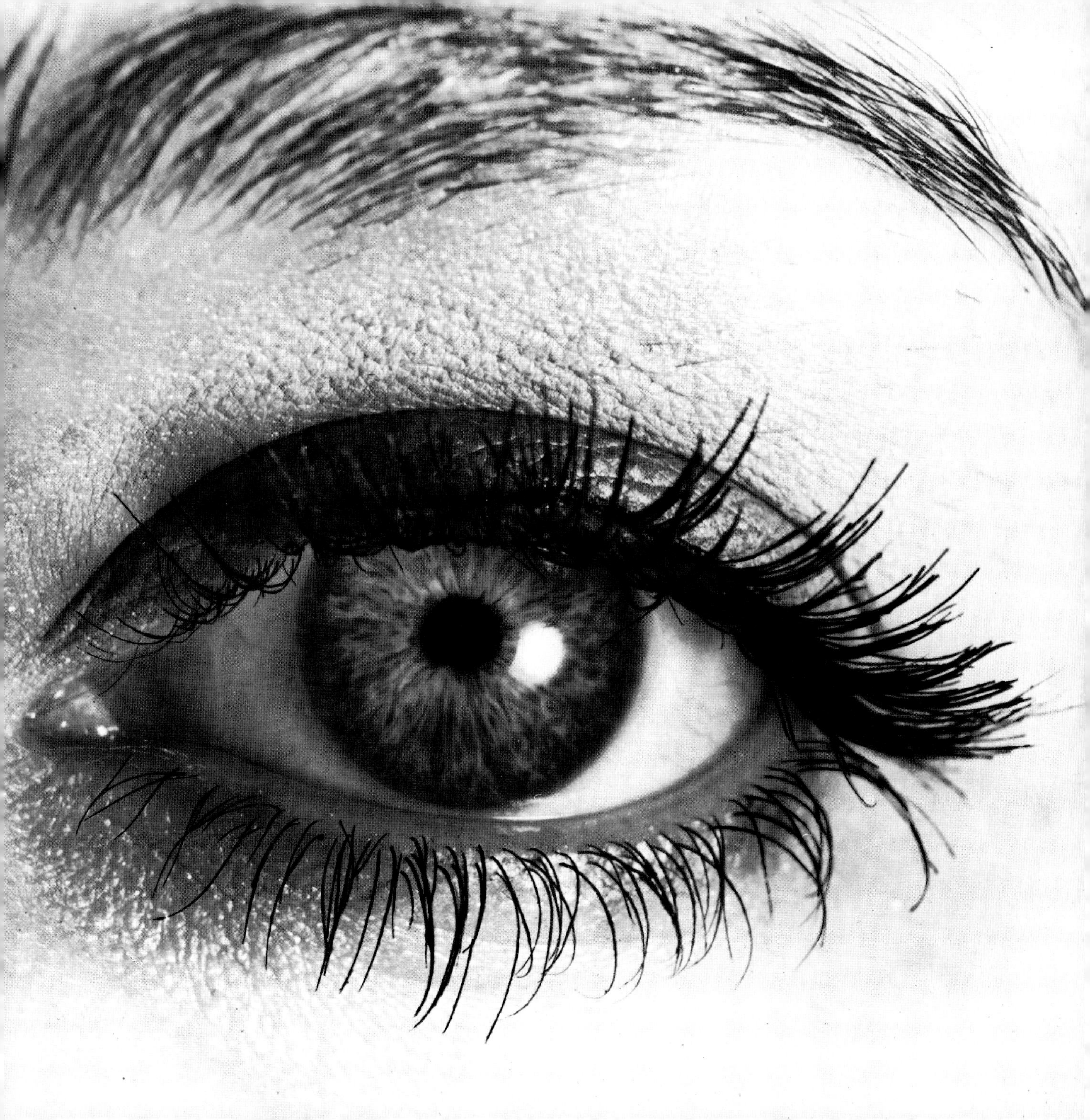

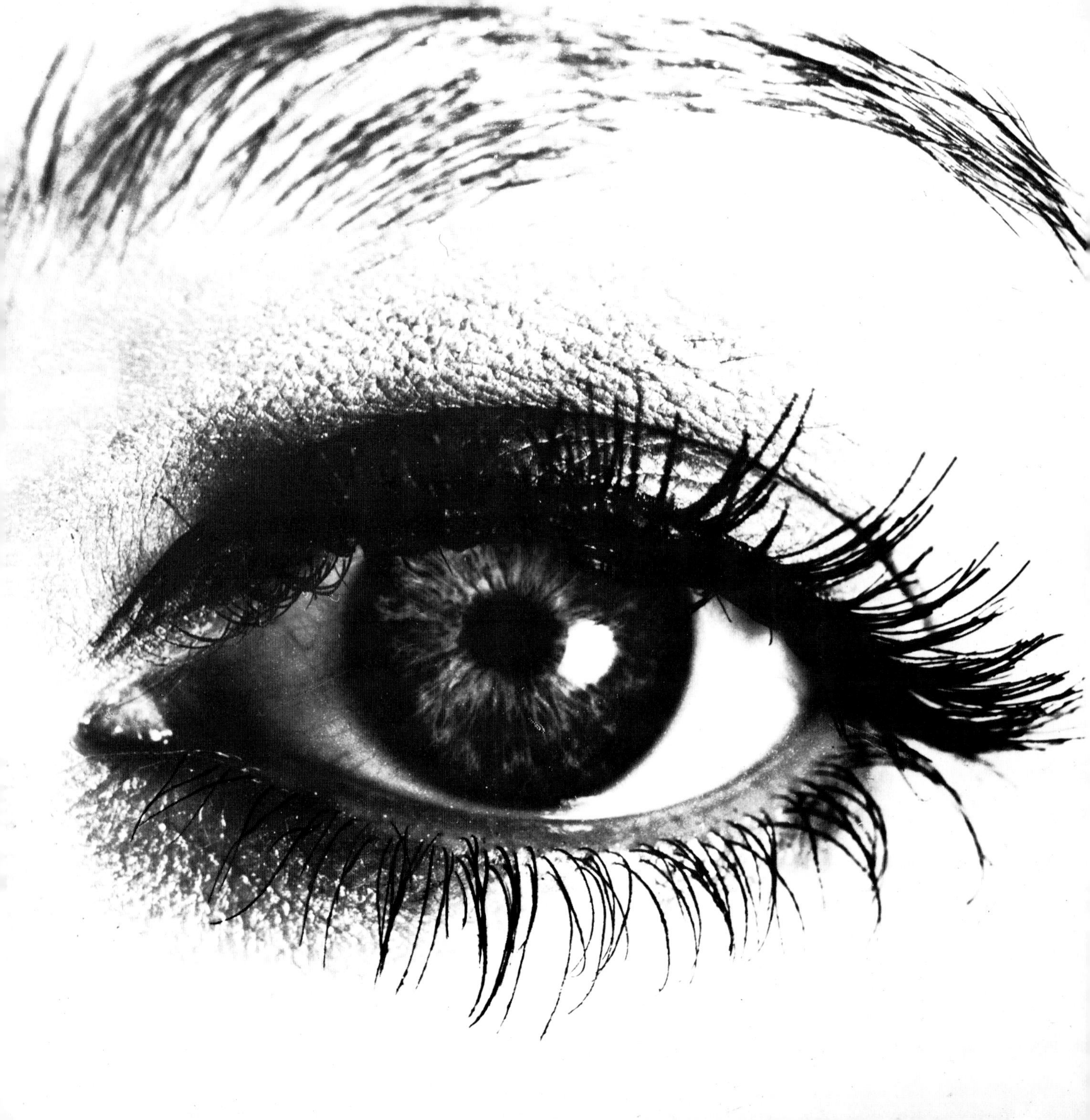

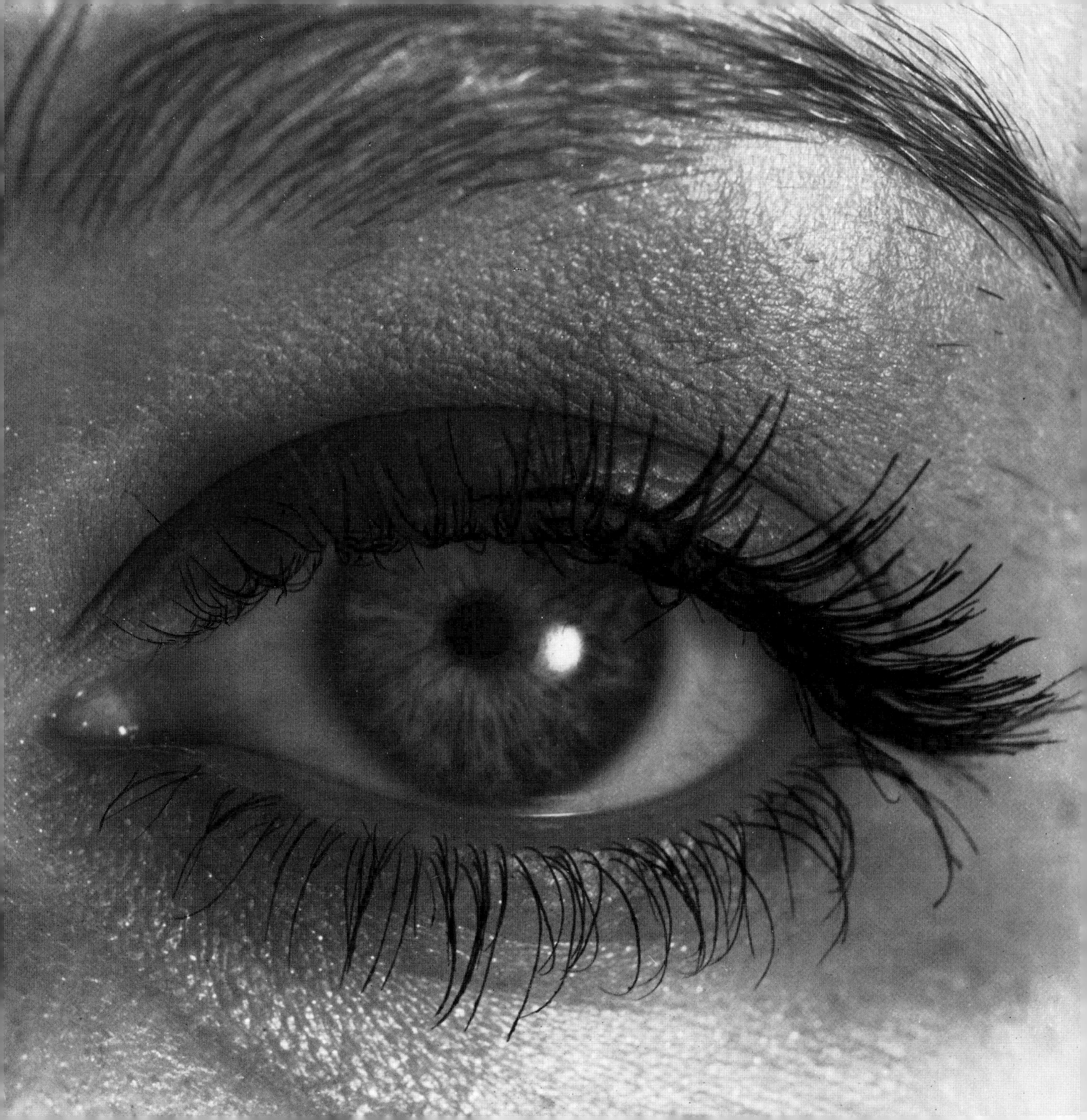

Continuous-Tone Enlargement, Negative

A further possibility of changing the tonal structure of a picture is to reverse its gray tones into the negative.

Procedure

(1) Position negative in enlarger.
(2) Optical copy onto continuous-tone print film (you obtain a positive).
(3) Position positive in enlarger.
(4) Determine image area and sharpness.
(5) Put print paper on easel.
(6) Find exposure time, and expose.
(7) Develop, stop, fix, wash, and dry.

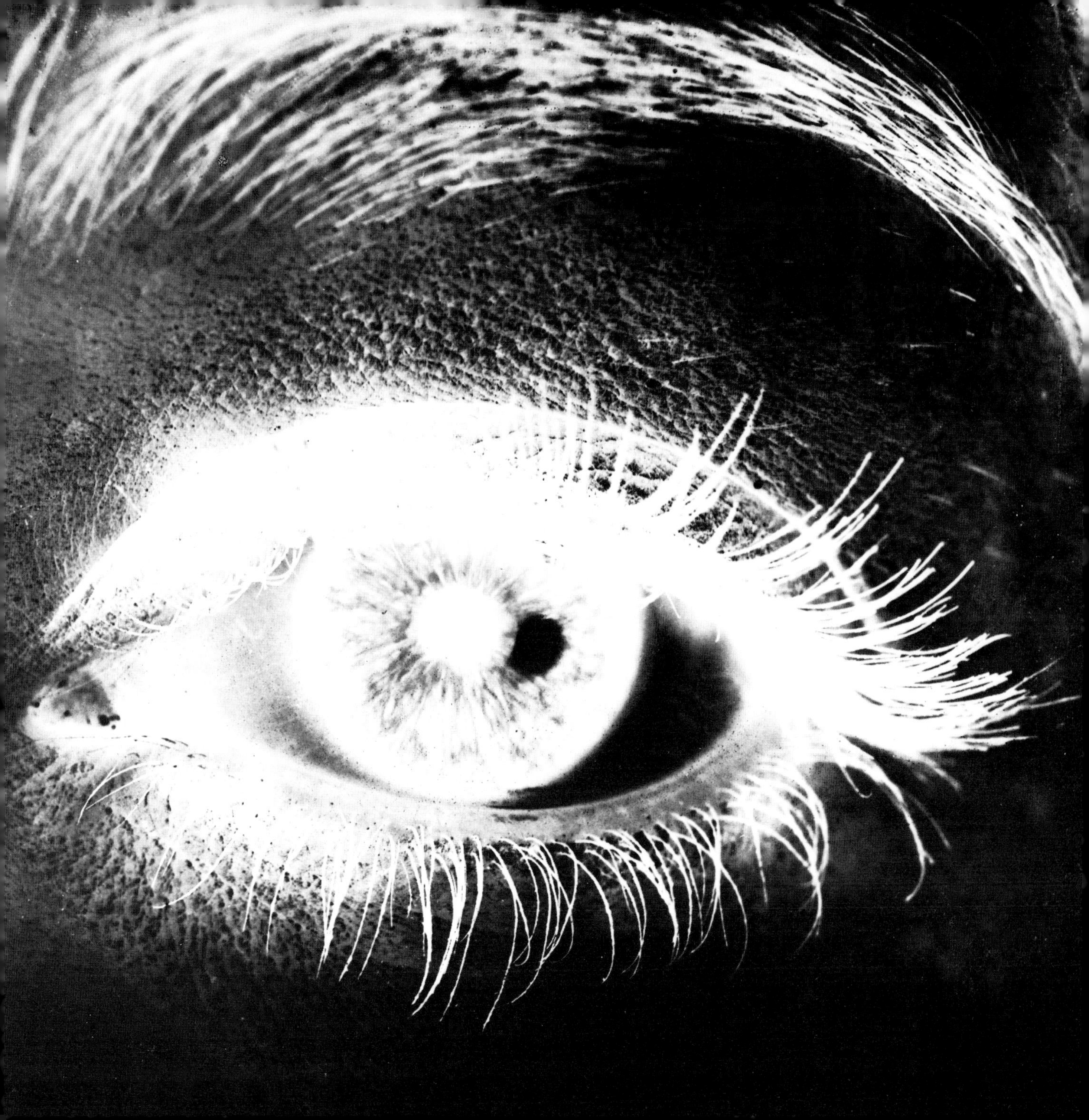

Continuous-Tone Enlargement, Unsharp

A picture which is intentionally copied unsharp appears smaller to the image of an optical soft design.

Procedure

(1) Position negative in enlarger.
(2) Determine degree of desired unsharpness.
(3) Expose, develop, etc.

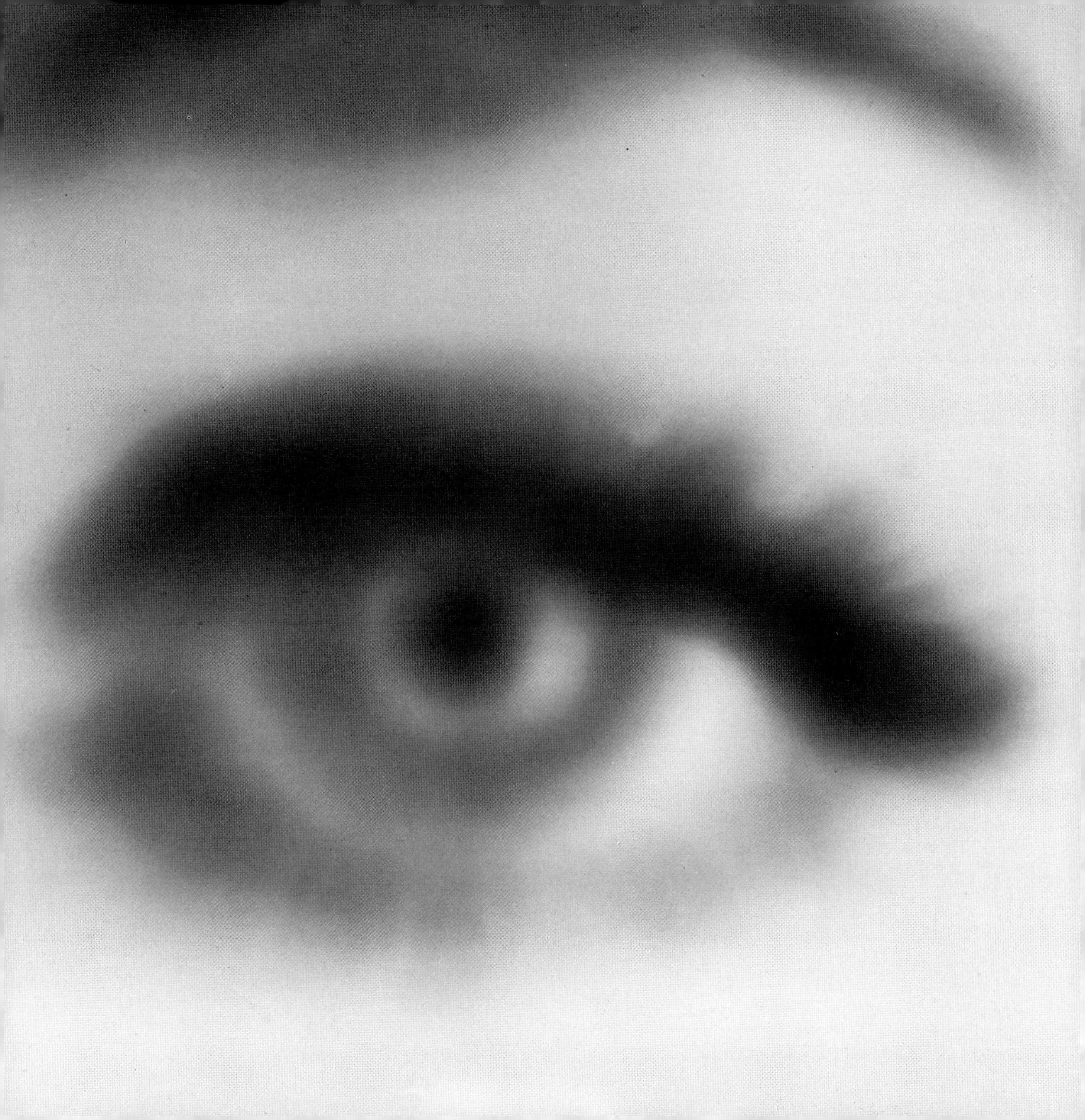

Motion

Procedure

(1) Position negative in enlarger.
(2) Determine image area and sharpness.
(3) Position photo paper.
(4) During exposure move photo paper or change distance of enlarger from easel.
(5) Develop, stop, fix, wash, and dry.

Depending on the subject and the exposure, motion can be produced or even increased by a simple technique. During exposure, the enlarger is moved up or down.

Another motion effect is easily accomplished by moving the photo paper laterally.

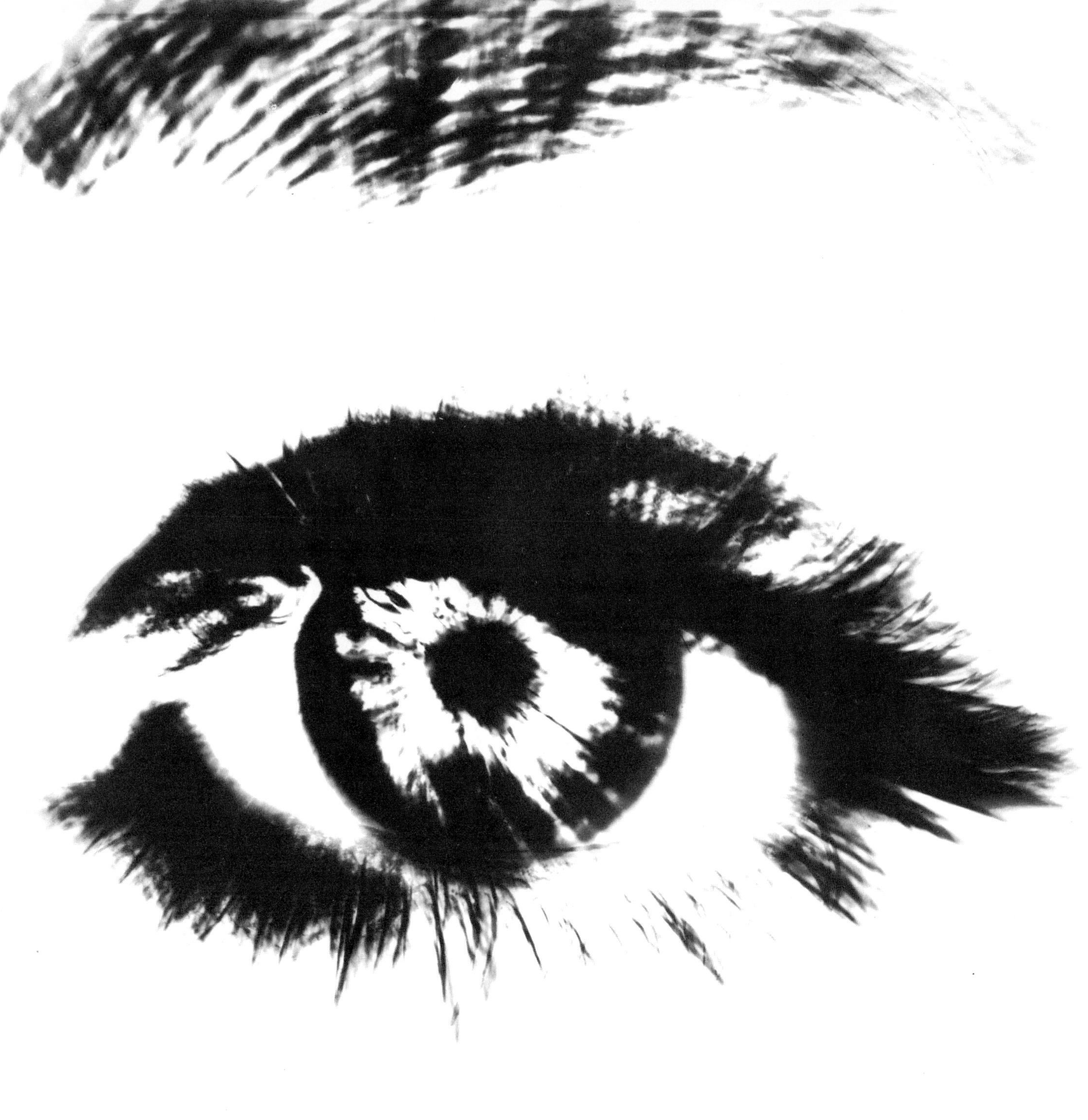

Multiple Exposures

Multiple exposures are made in different ways: by enlargements in varying ratios, by repositioning the subject vertically or horizontally, or by consecutive copying of different images.

The example on the opposite page shows the representation of the same subject in different ratios of enlargement.

When using this technique, it is important not to diminish the inherent form of the subject matter.

Procedure

(1) *Determine image area and sharpness for first exposure (larger copy).*
(2) *Position photo paper.*
(3) *Expose.*
(4) *Change image section to a smaller size; possibly move photo paper.*
(5) *Expose, develop, fix, wash, and dry.*

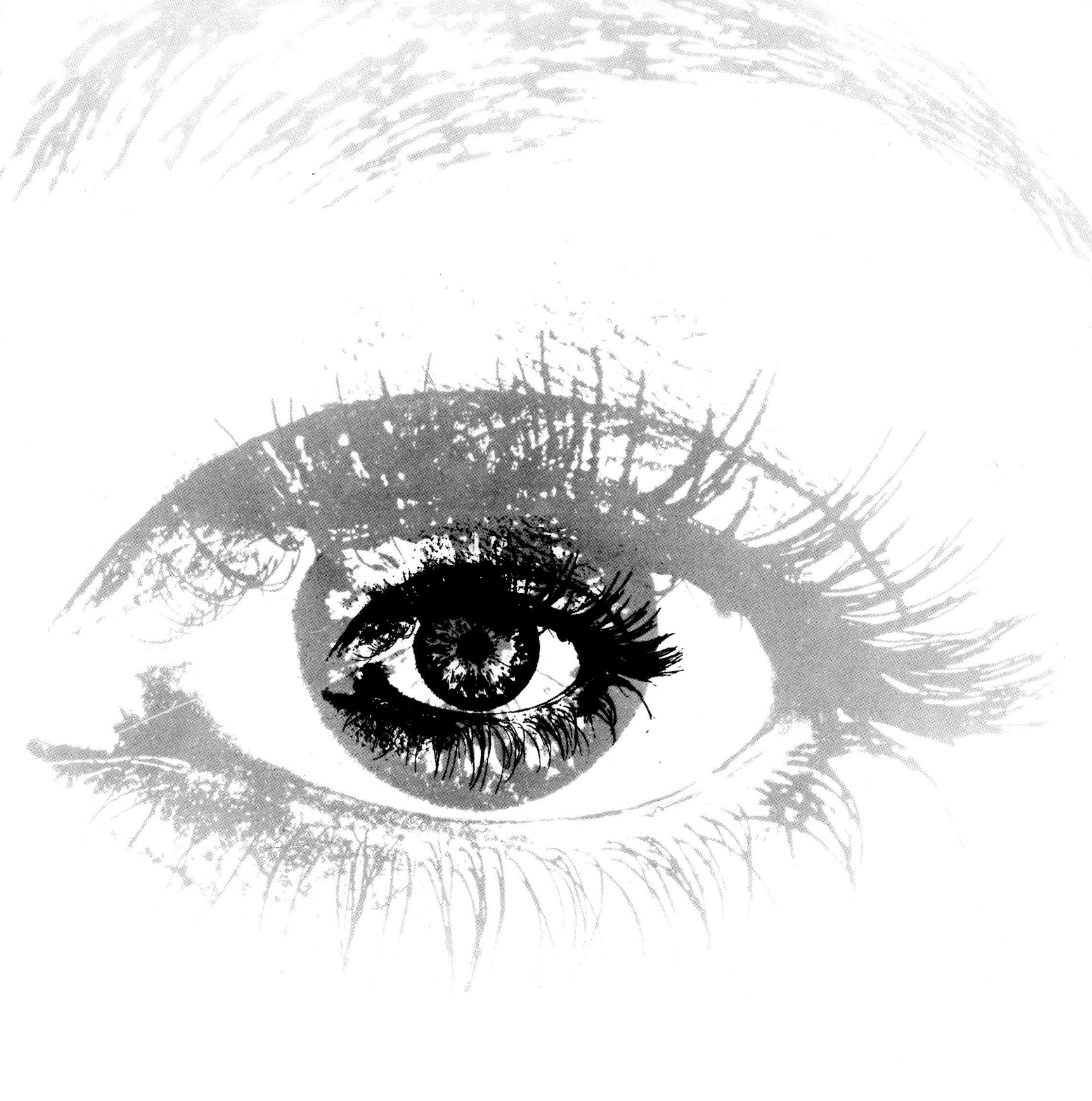

Soft Contouring

By using light diffraction, the normal contour sharpness of the copy is prevented. One obtains an image with washed-out, unsharp contours and outlines.

When soft contouring a copy, it is observed that the larger the aperture of the enlarger lens, the softer the pictorial effect.

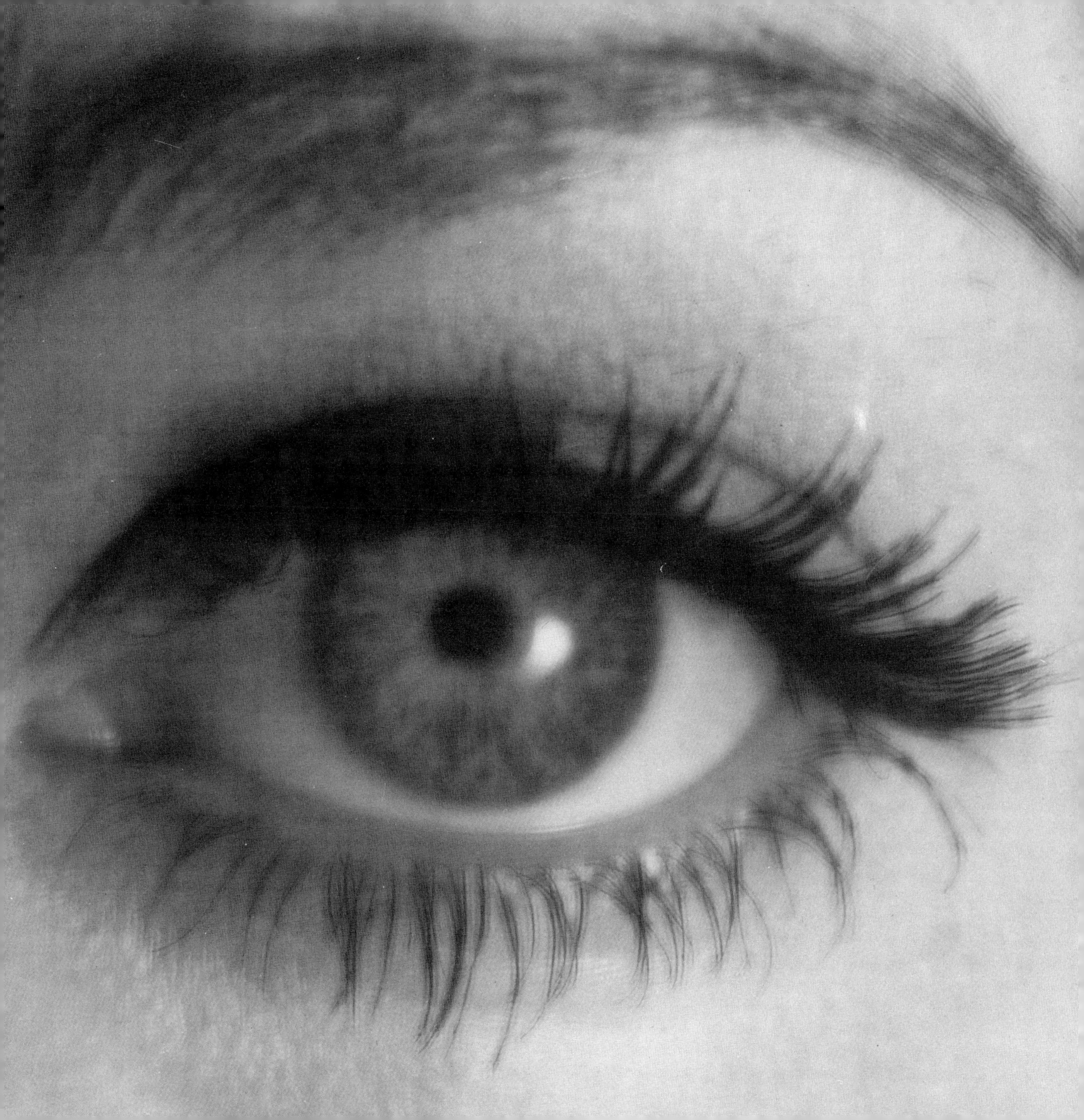

Greased Glass Plate

Smear a little vaseline with the fingertips in lines or circles on a glass plate. The prepared glass plate is held closely under the enlarger lens to form unsharp zones which overlap the directed image light beams.

With different grease thicknesses and distances to the enlarger lens, many variations can be created.

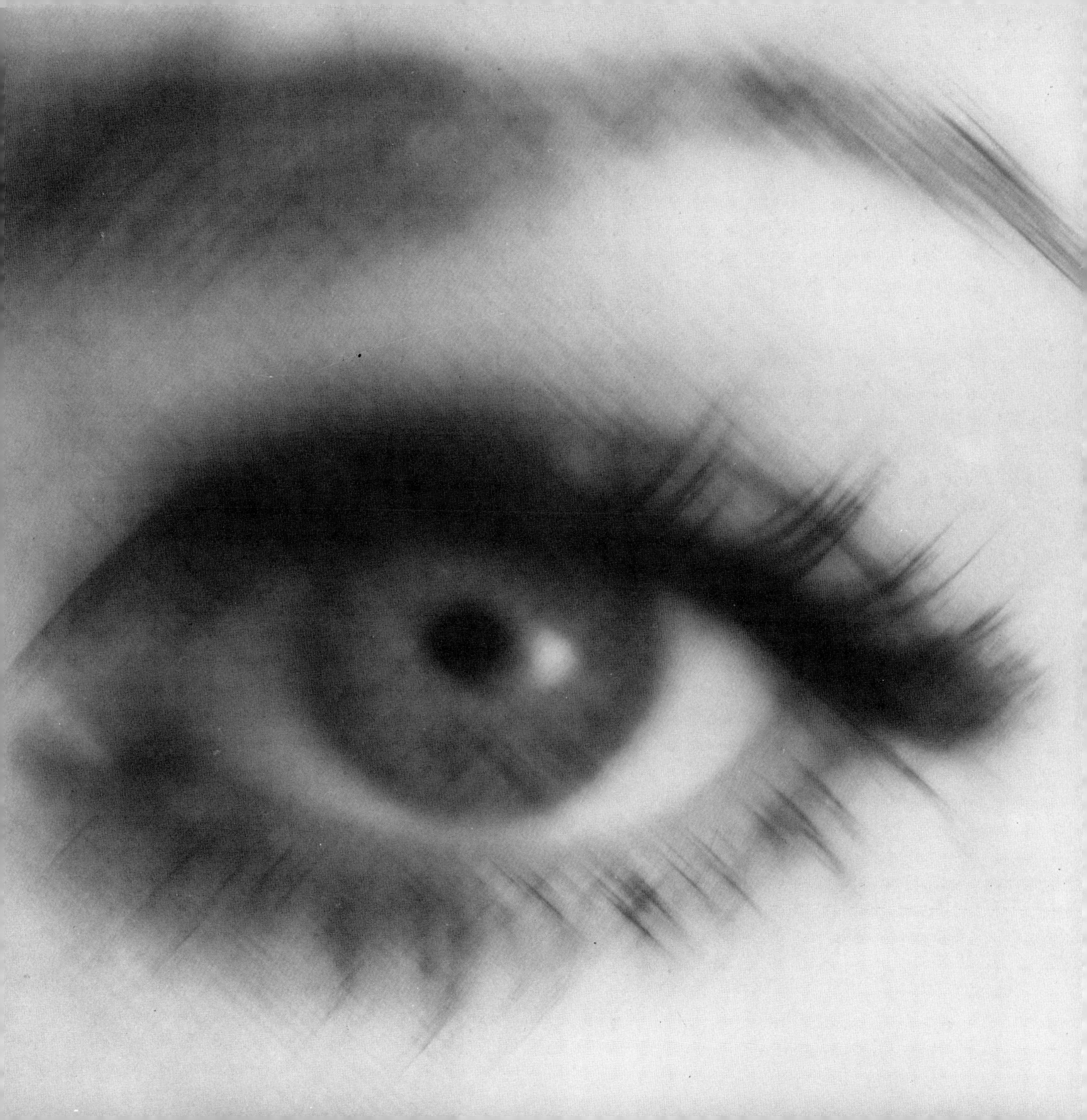

Repetitive Copying, Positive

<table>
<tr><td>

Procedure

(1) *Position negative in enlarger.*

(2) *Determine image area and sharpness.*

(3) *Put extra hard paper or lithographic film on easel.*

(4) *Expose, develop, stop, fix, wash, and dry.*

(5) *Place result with emulsion down onto extra-hard paper. Press onto copy frame and expose with enlarger.*

(6) *Develop, stop, fix, wash, and dry. (Negative enlargement is achieved.)*

(7) *With negative enlargement, repeat same procedure.*

(8) *Develop, stop, fix, wash, and dry. Result positive.*

(9) *An intensification of the effect is achieved by further recopying.*

</td></tr>
</table>

Repetitive copying is one of.the most widely used photographic techniques because of the poster-like quality of the photographic results. Repetitive copying is easily recognized by its clear, hard black-and-white contrast. All gray values of the continuous-tone subject are rendered either into black or white image areas with this procedure.

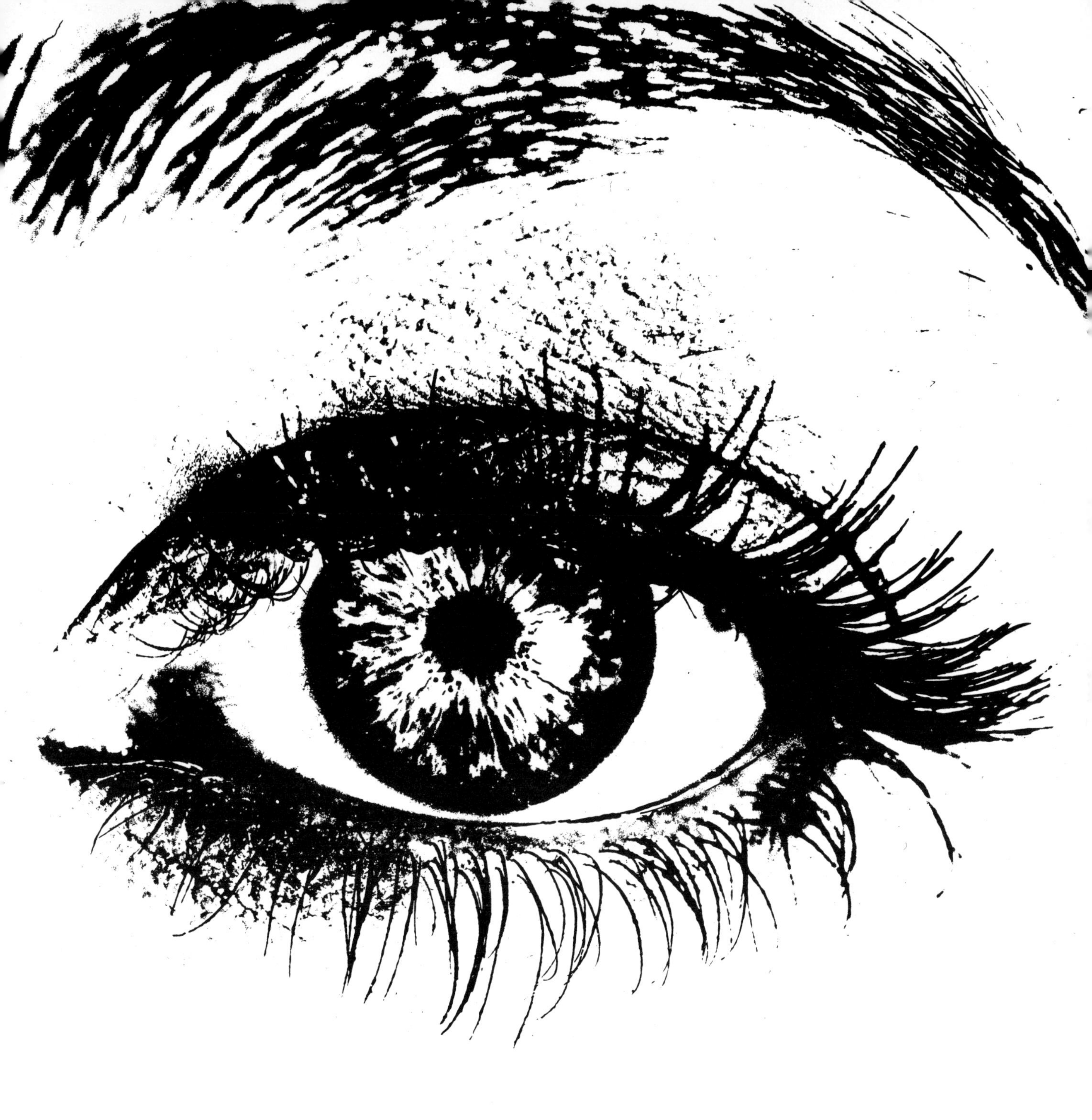

Repetitive Copying, Negative

According to the desired effect, one can also use the negative form of repetitive copy procedure. For a correctly placed representation of a recopied negative subject, the original negative should be placed into the enlarger carrier in a reversed position.

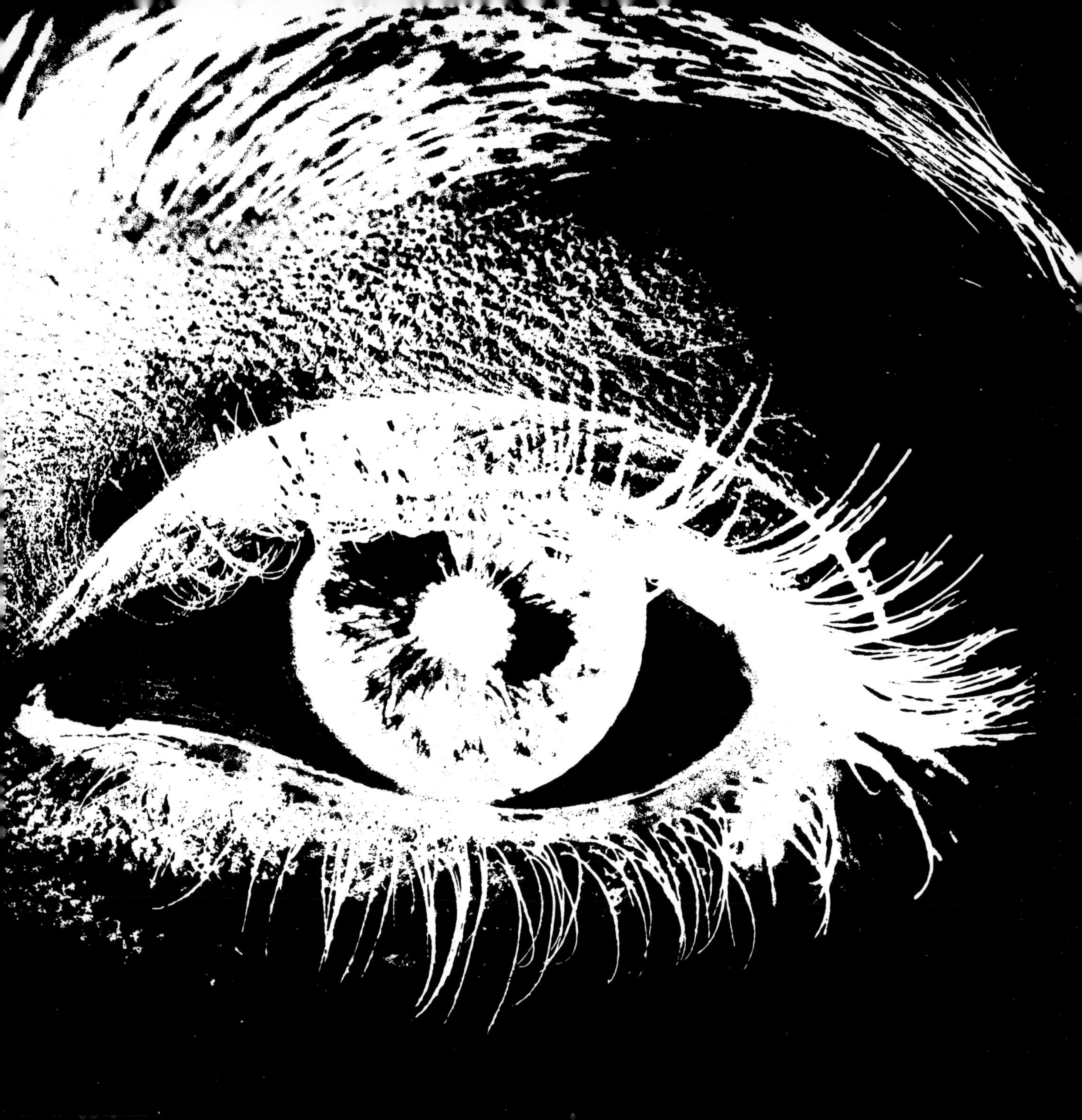

Black-and-White Tonal Separation

Procedure

(1) Put registration markers on original negative.
(2) Copy internegatives of different gray densities.
(3) Mount in register the dense, less dense and almost transparent negatives to a film pack with tape.
(4) Position in enlarger.
(5) Determine image area and sharpness.
(6) Expose (or expose each negative individually and in register) onto photo paper.
(7) Develop, stop, fix, wash, and dry.

The separation of tonal steps is a laboratory technique which slices a picture into a few density intervals. Differently exposed film positives are copied from the original negative. They are copied with identical exposure times in contact onto film material to make negatives. When mounted on top of each other in register and enlarged on normal graded paper, a tonal separation is achieved.

A different procedure: the same result is produced by single exposures of the different negatives directly onto copy paper. Results: one white image area, one or several gray image areas, and one black image area.

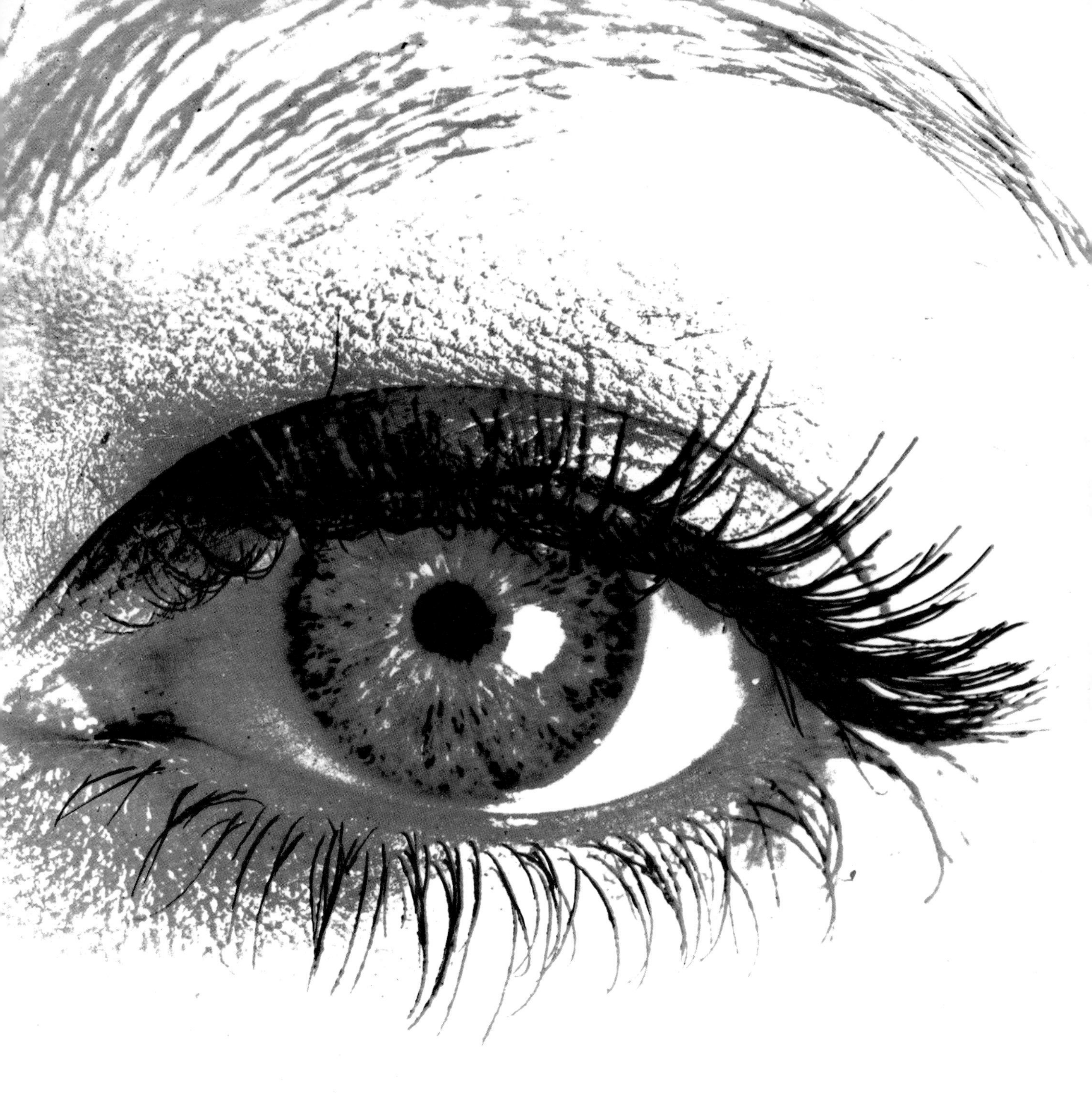

Relief

Procedure

(1) *Put registration markers on original negative.*
(2) *Copy a positive from the original negative (matching density).*
(3) *Remount slightly out of register.*
(4) *Position in enlarger.*
(5) *Determine image area and sharpness.*
(6) *Copy onto normal photo paper.*
(7) *Expose, develop, stop, fix, wash, and dry.*

If a negative and a positive are mounted on top of each other but slightly out of register, the effect of a flat relief is obtained. Conditions for the success of this technique are continuous-tone negatives and positives which show similar densities and gradations.

Placed on top of each other, negative and positive result in a continuously gray area by which neither dominates as image. By slight lateral motion of the image area out of register, the relief effect is produced.

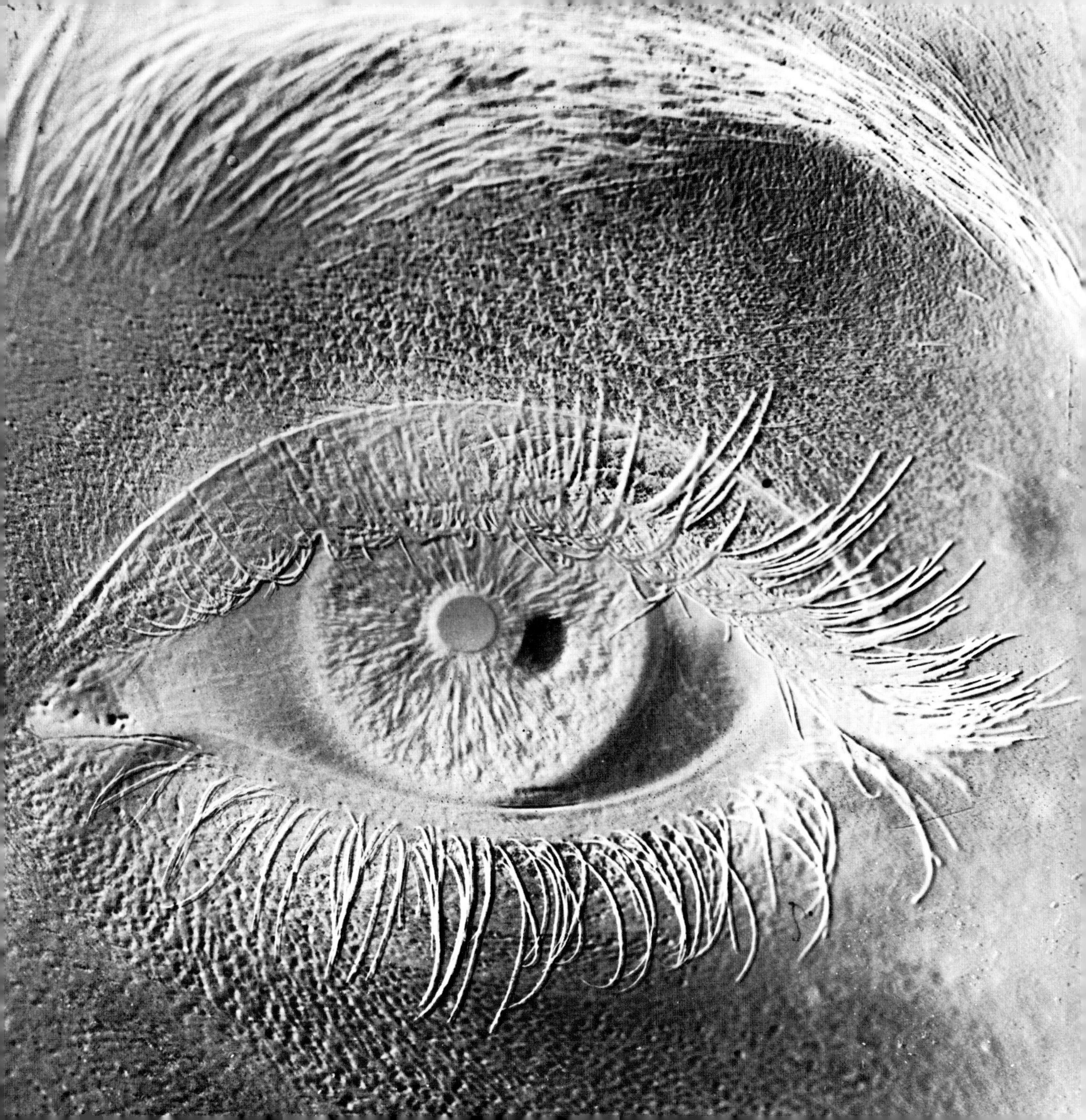

Linear Relief

Procedure

(1) Same procedure as for
continuous-tone relief.
(2) Use of repetitively copied film
negative and positive.

With the same technical working procedure as used for continuous-tone relief, a completely different result can be achieved. The relief effect is obtained by a shadow-like line contour. The only difference from the continuous-tone technique is that instead of the continuous-tone negative and positive, a repetitively copied film negative and a repetitively copied film positive are used here.

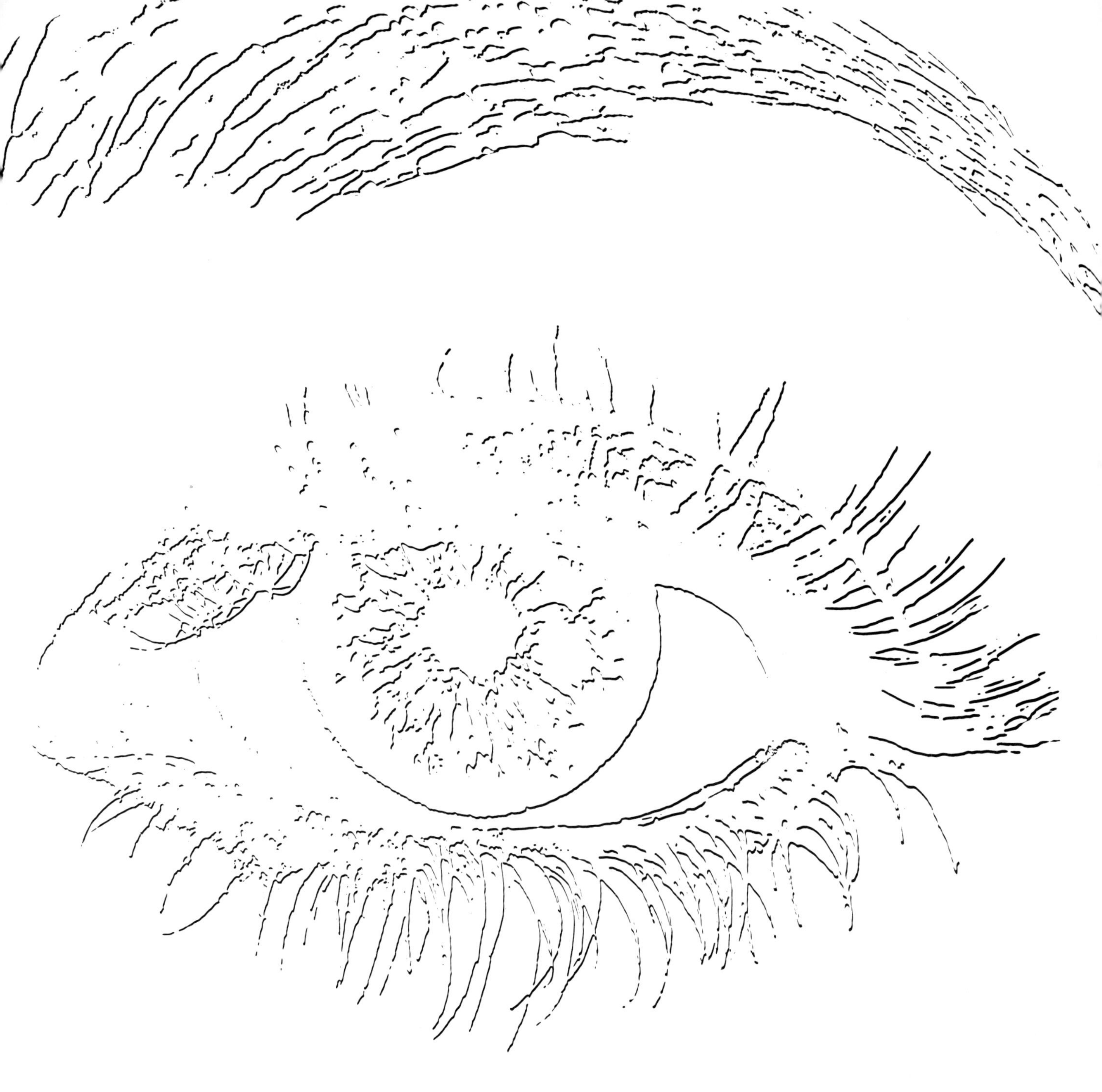

Pseudosolarization

Procedure

(1) *Enlargement on grade six extra-hard paper.*
(2) *Beginning of development—50%.*
(3) *Short exposure with diffused light source in developer tray.*
(4) *Develop completely.*
(5) *From this negative result a first copy on extra-hard paper gives the first positive solarization step.*
(6) *Repeating the procedure with the first result gives a further increase of the solarization effect.*

The solarization process shows a partial reversal of the gray densities from the positive to the negative. This effect can be produced by a second exposure which is done during the development of the print. This second exposure and the ensuing contoured development renders the image black wherever there are white image areas. Between those positive and negative image areas, light contouring lines appear which are characteristic of the solarization effect.

Page 39: First solarization step, positive.
Page 40: Second solarization step, negative.
Page 41: Second solarization step, positive.

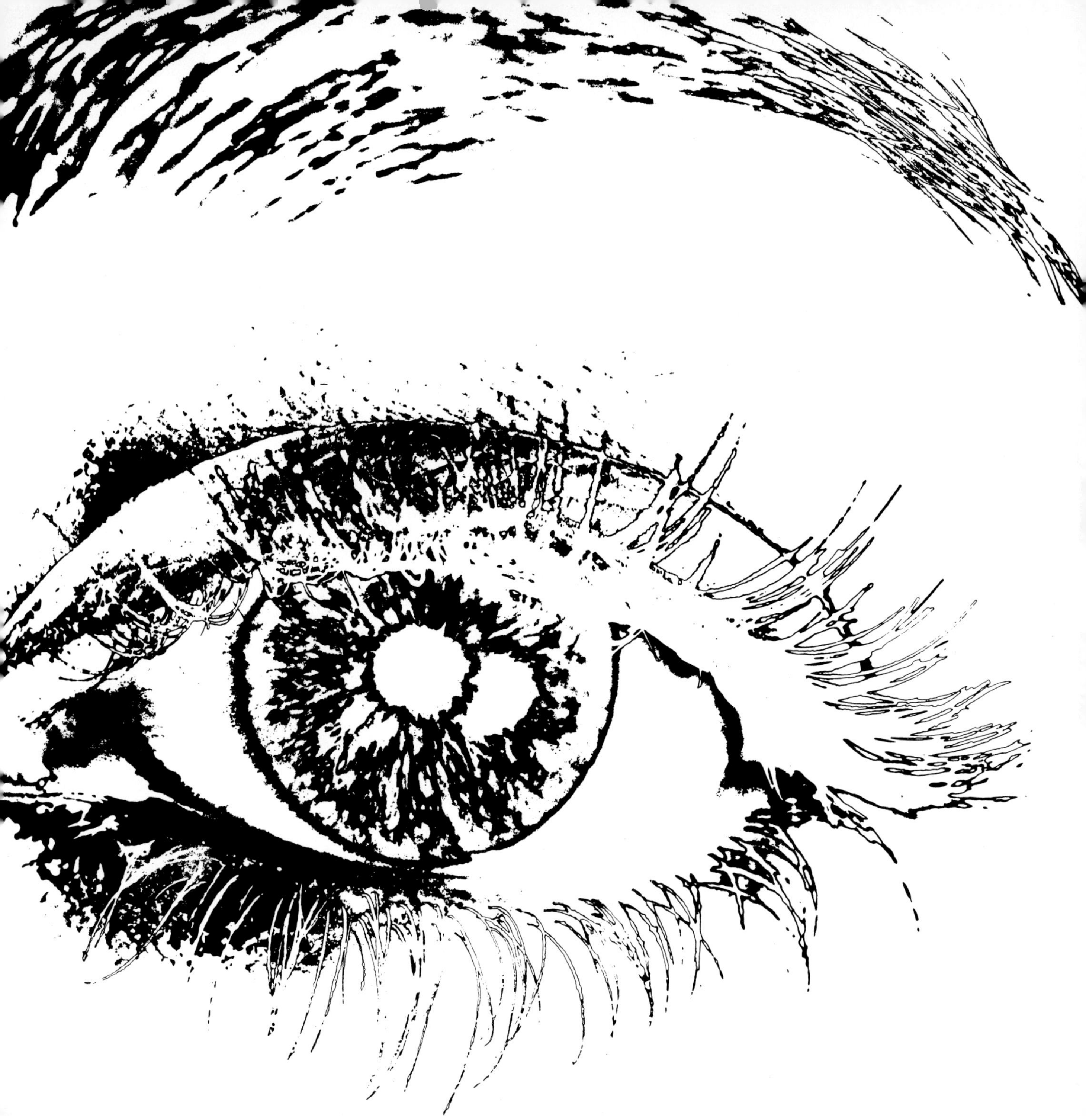

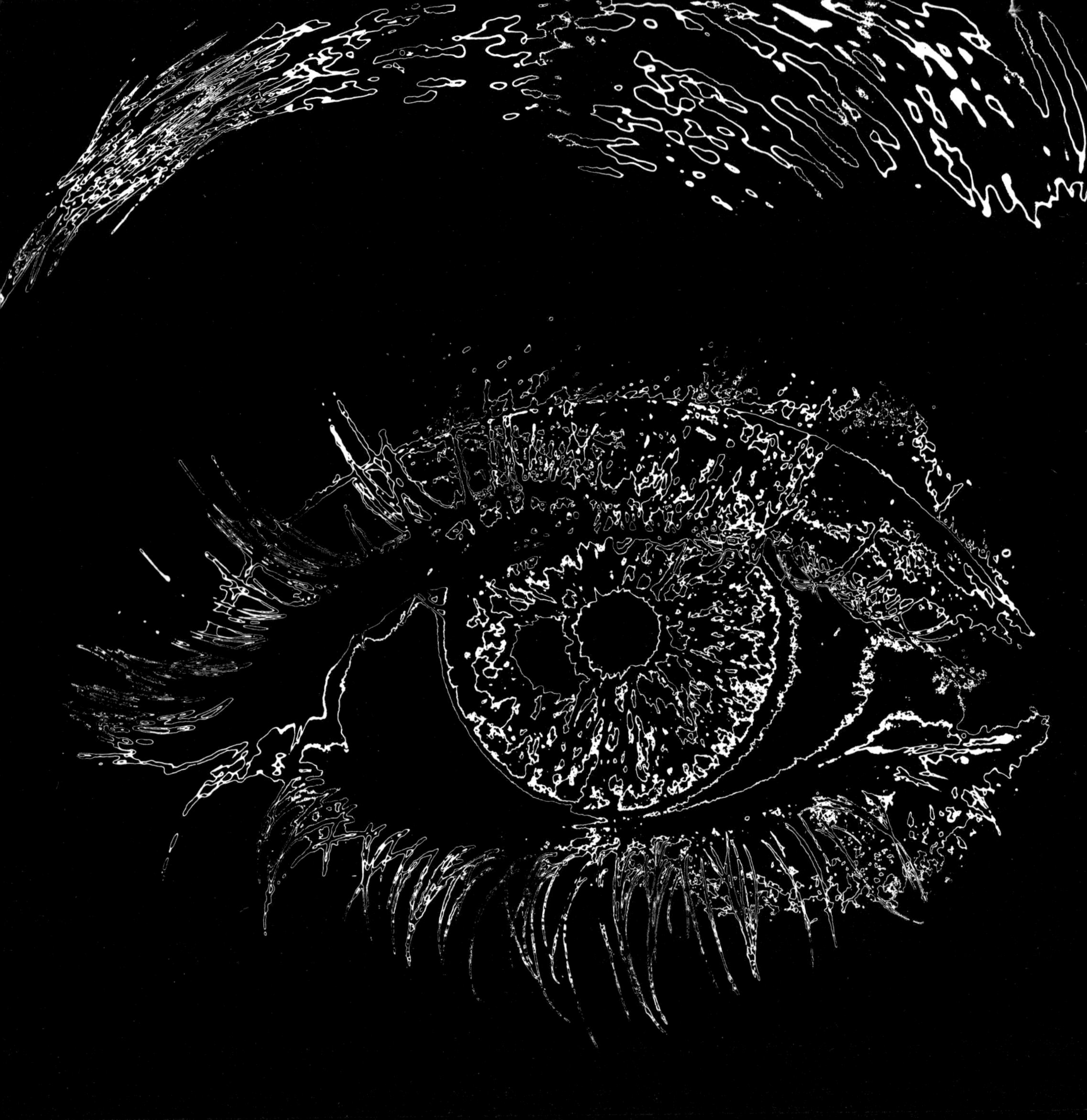

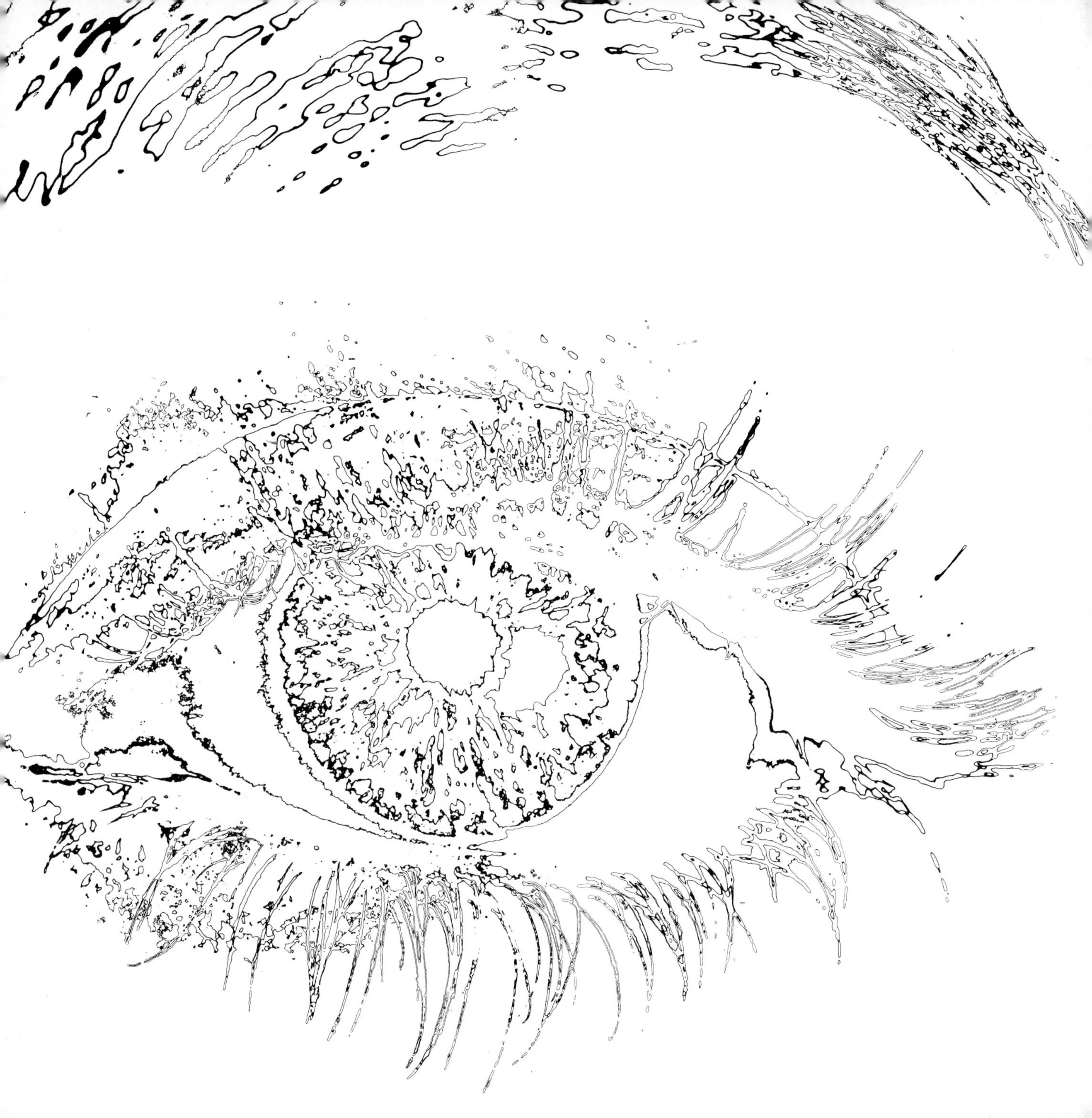

Lines of Equal Density

<table>
<tr><td>

Procedure

(1) *Copy from the negative a positive of equal density and gray values.*

(2) *Mount in register, emulsions apart.*

(3) *Put hard-copying documentation film into easel, emulsion to exposure source.*

(4) *Place positive/negative package on top (positive mask upward).*

(5) *Close exposure frame and place on rotating disc.*

(6) *Place light point source (enlarger or projector) at a distance of 10 to 12 feet at a 45 degree angle to the rotating disc.*

(7) *During rotation, expose 20 to 30 seconds.*

(8) *Develop 2 to 3 minutes in lithographic developer.*

(9) *From the obtained positive, copy a contact negative.*

(10) *From the negative, make an enlargement onto extra-hard paper.*

</td></tr>
</table>

When lines of equal density are used, an image appears which is similar to an india ink drawing. However, it does not lose the photographic character of the original.

From the original negative a positive mask is copied which has similar density and gray values. Negative and positive are mounted in register, so that an even dark gray area is obtained. It is important that the emulsion sides of both of them should not be in contact.

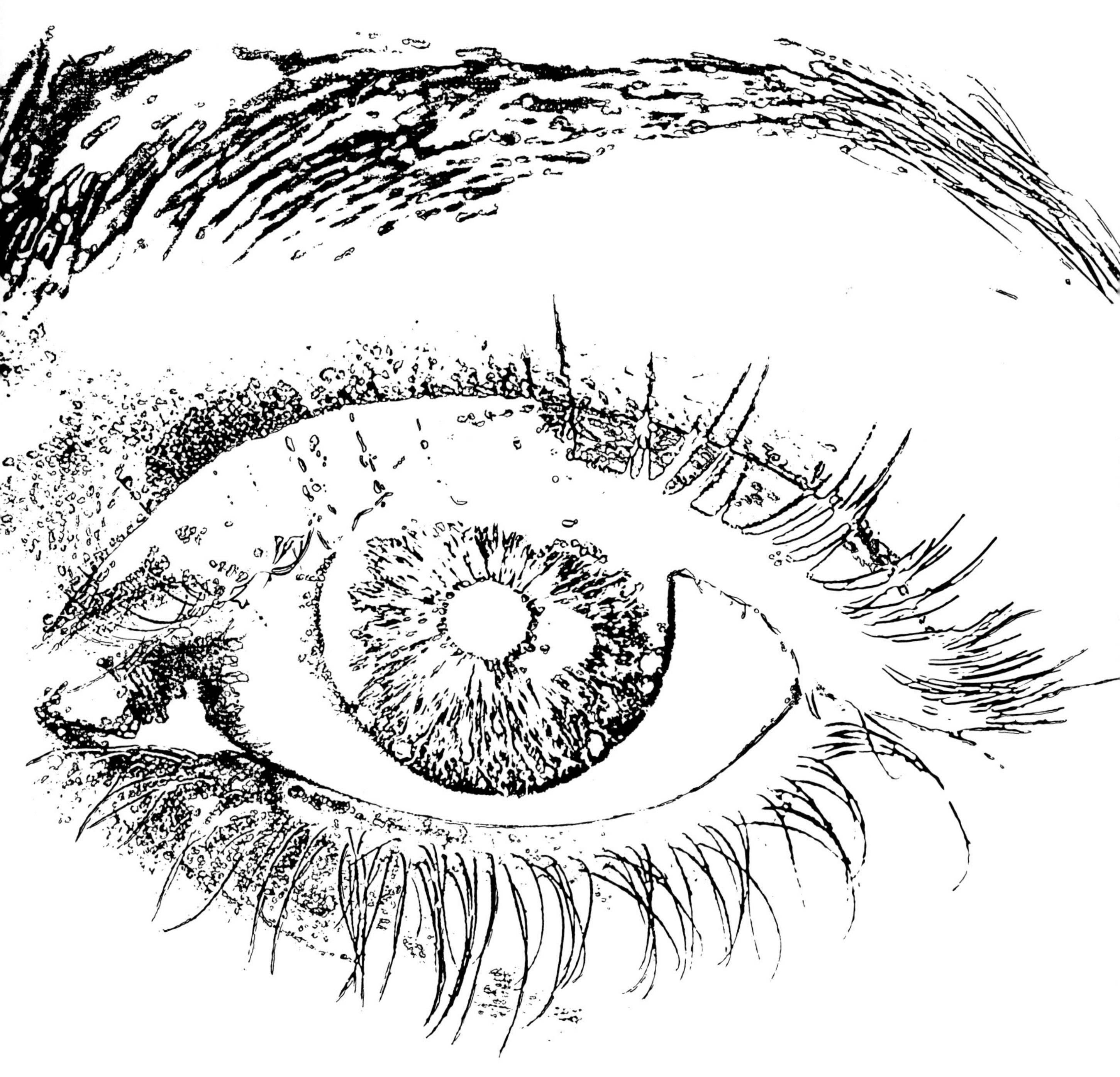

Agfacontour

Procedure

(1) From a continuous-tone original negative, using a gray wedge, lines of equal density of the first order are produced in contact copy. They are separations of different tonal values of the original negative. It is recommended to use a gray scale.

(2) Recopying of the equidensity lines of the first order onto Agfacontour film using a .20—.40 yellow filter.

(3) Lines of equal density of the second order are obtained. There are only fine lines left which contour the former gray areas like an ink drawing.

(4) An enlargement of these second order lines is made on extra-hard paper.

Agfacontour film is a photographic film material which can separate images into line structures of equal densities. This lab technique opens new possibilities of graphic forms. By means of abstraction and concentration of pictorial contents into a few lines or areas, certain graphical effects are realized.

It is recommended to follow the manufacturers directions when using this rather complicated technique.

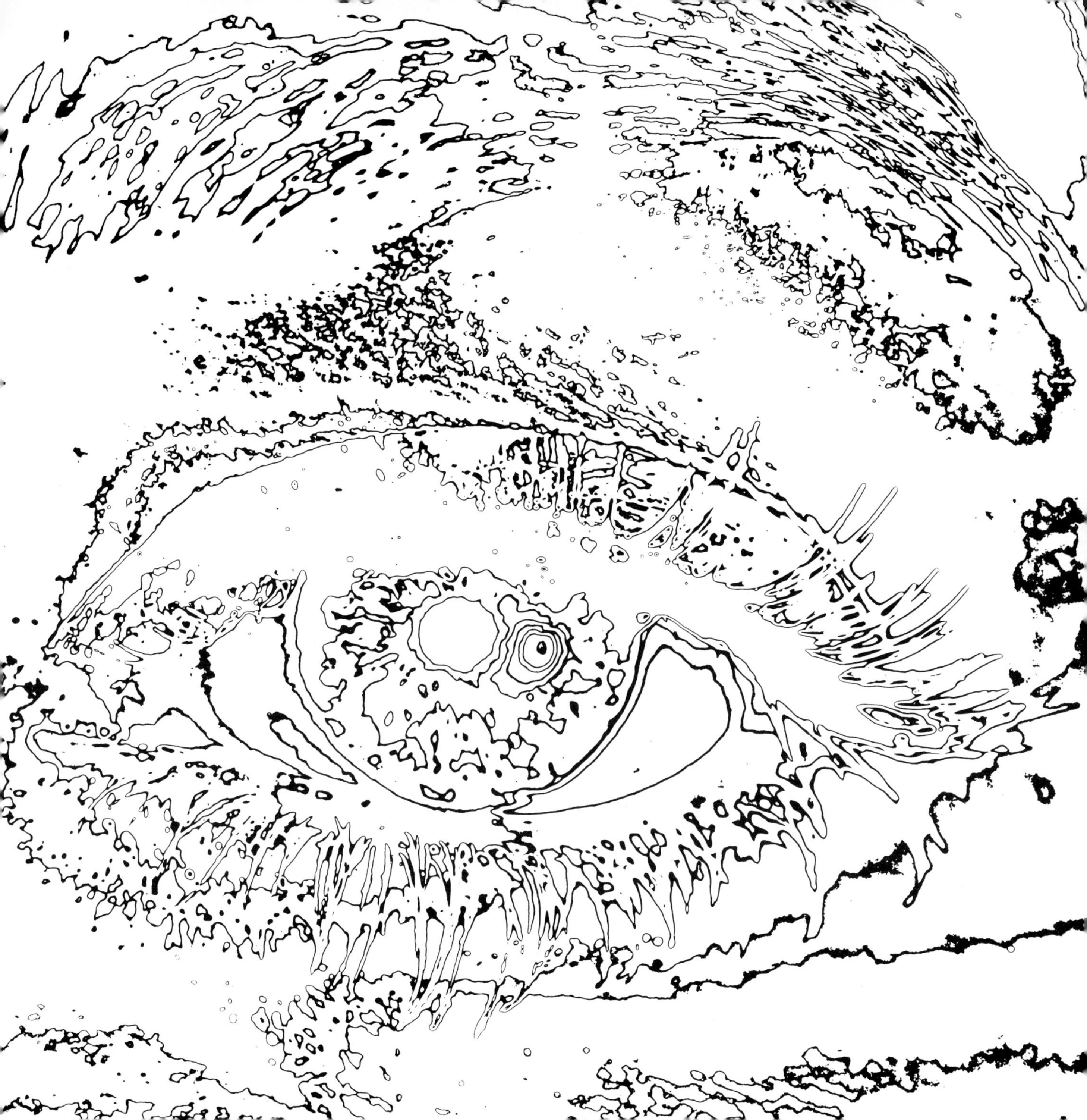

Screening

When screening a photographic subject, all gray values are changed into lines or dots of varied size and area. This type of screening is used by printing houses to get photographic pictures ready for printing. With proper enlargement of the screen, interesting graphic effects can be brought about.

If it is desired to transform an image into visible screen structures, one can order a preferably high resolution screen negative from a printing house or laboratory. From this negative, any kind of enlargements can be made in a smaller darkroom with just an enlarger.

Page 47: Dot screens (10 lines per mm).
Page 48: Line screen.
Page 49: Granular screen.

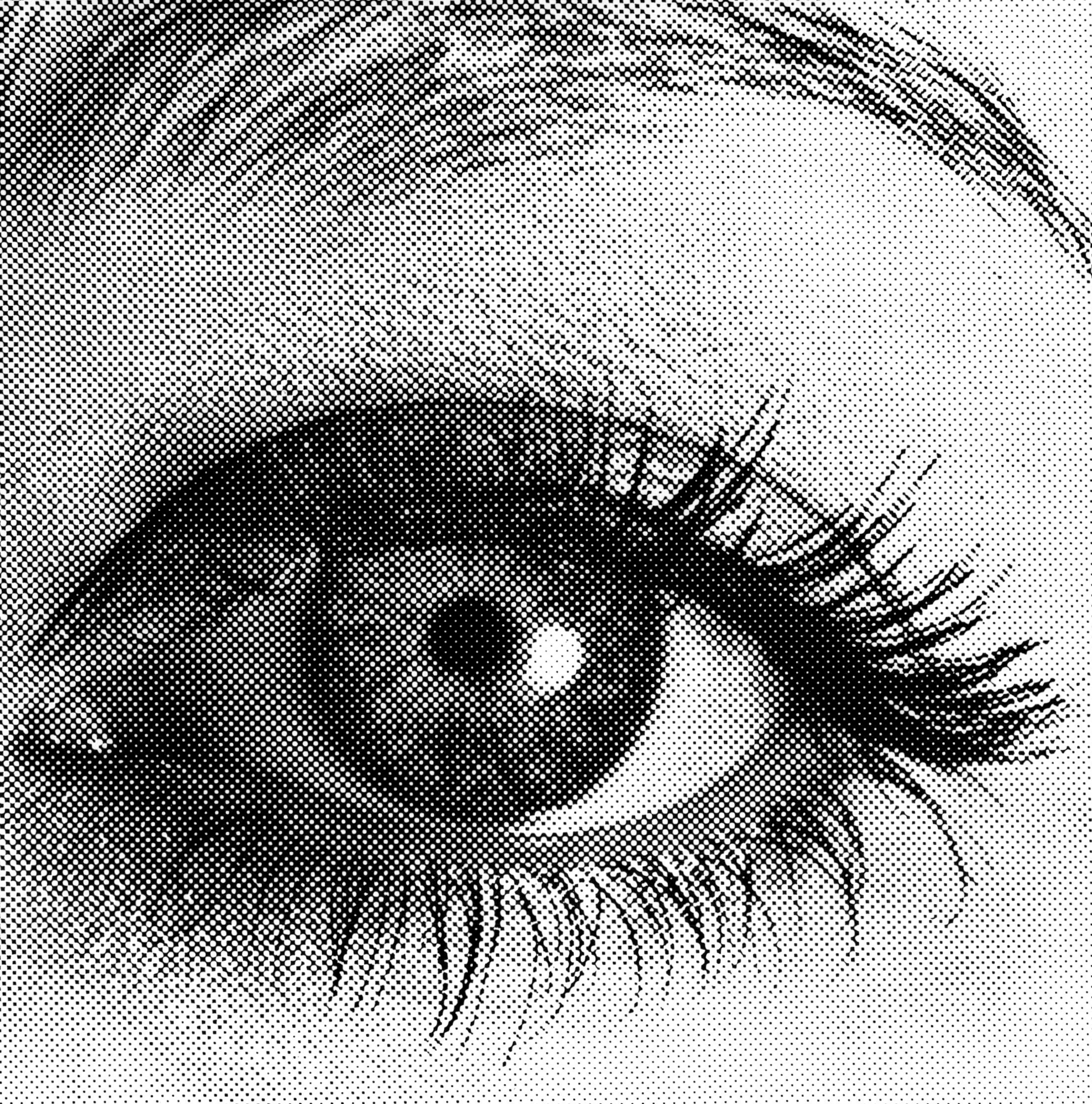

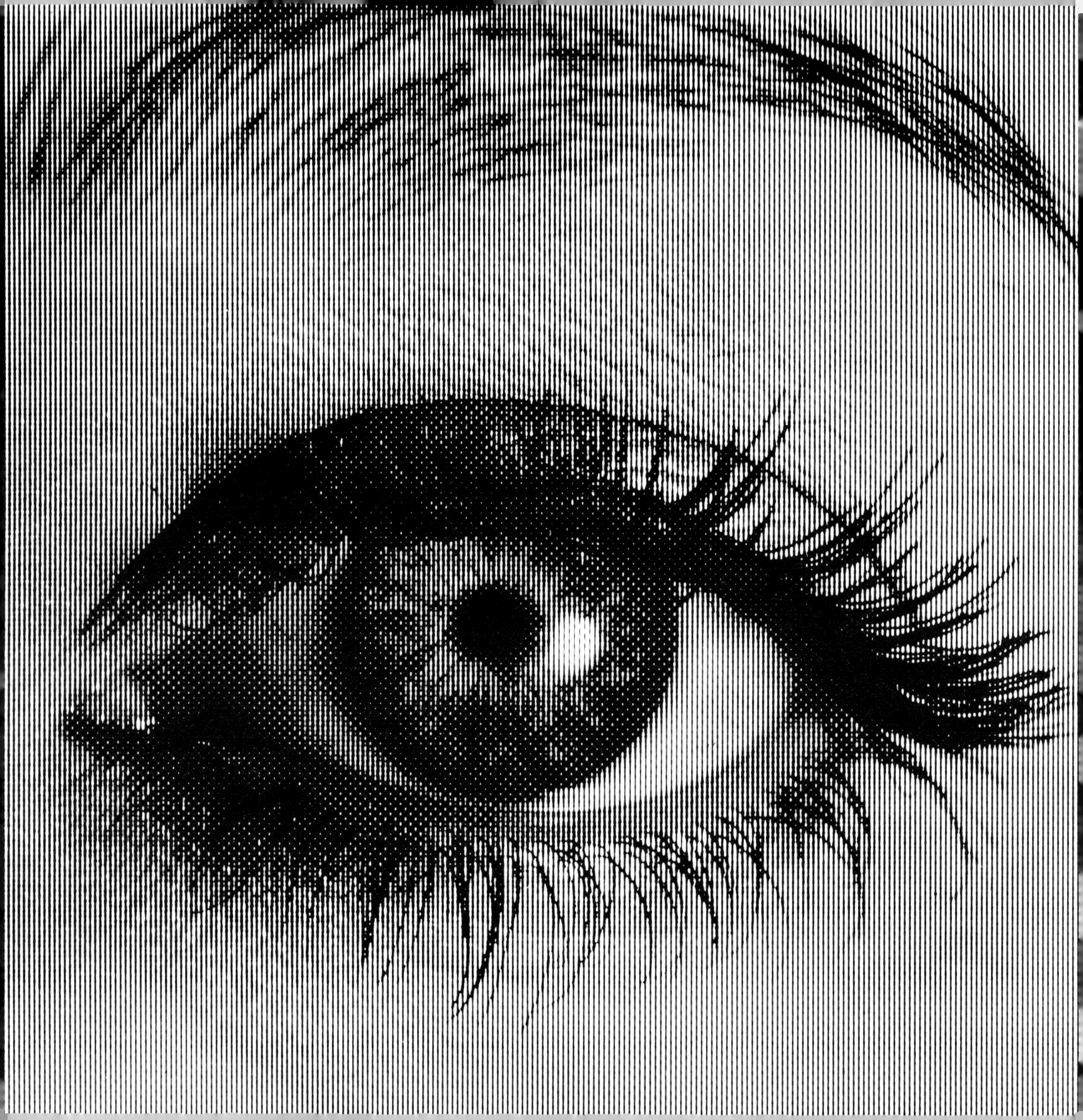

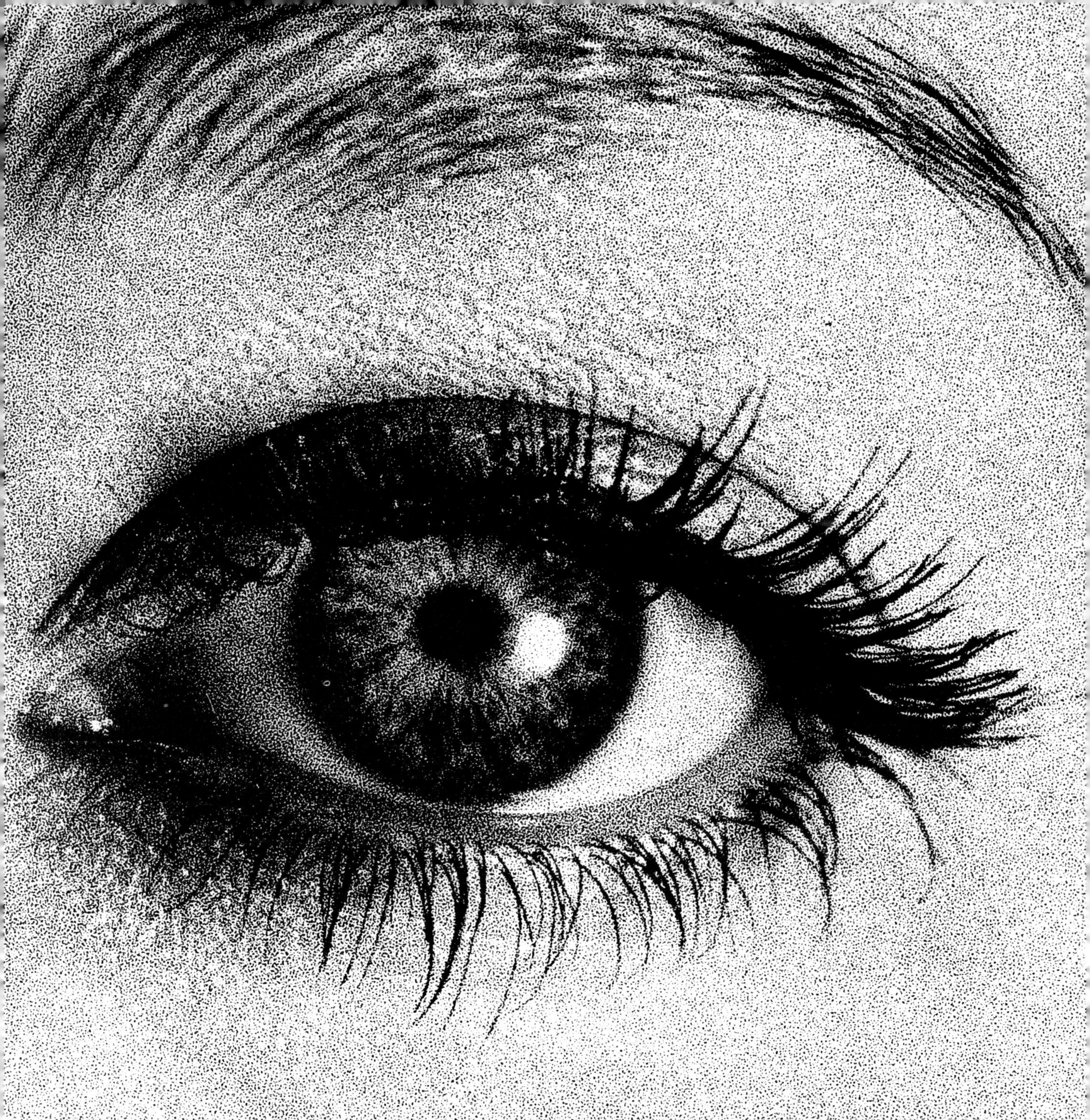

Screen Structures

Procedure

Part I

(1) Position negative in enlarger, determine image area and sharpness.

(2) Put screen mask or structure onto print paper and put on easel.

(3) Expose, develop, etc.

Part II

(1) Put negative in register with screen structure into enlarger.

(2) Expose, develop, stop, fix, wash, and dry.

Similar results to the ones on page 46 can be produced in a smaller laboratory. With this method it is not necessary to separate the image in lines or dots, but rather to superimpose a screen structure of different gray values. Transparent screen masks are available in many forms and shapes in graphic art supply stores. It is easy to either superimpose such a screen mask onto the print paper or to enlarge it together with the negative.

Furthermore, rilled glass, gauze, thin structured paper, etc., and even things like gravel, wood grain, brick walls, or foliage can be photographed and used.

Page 51: Coarse linen screen.
Page 52: Radial screen.
Page 53: Circular screen.

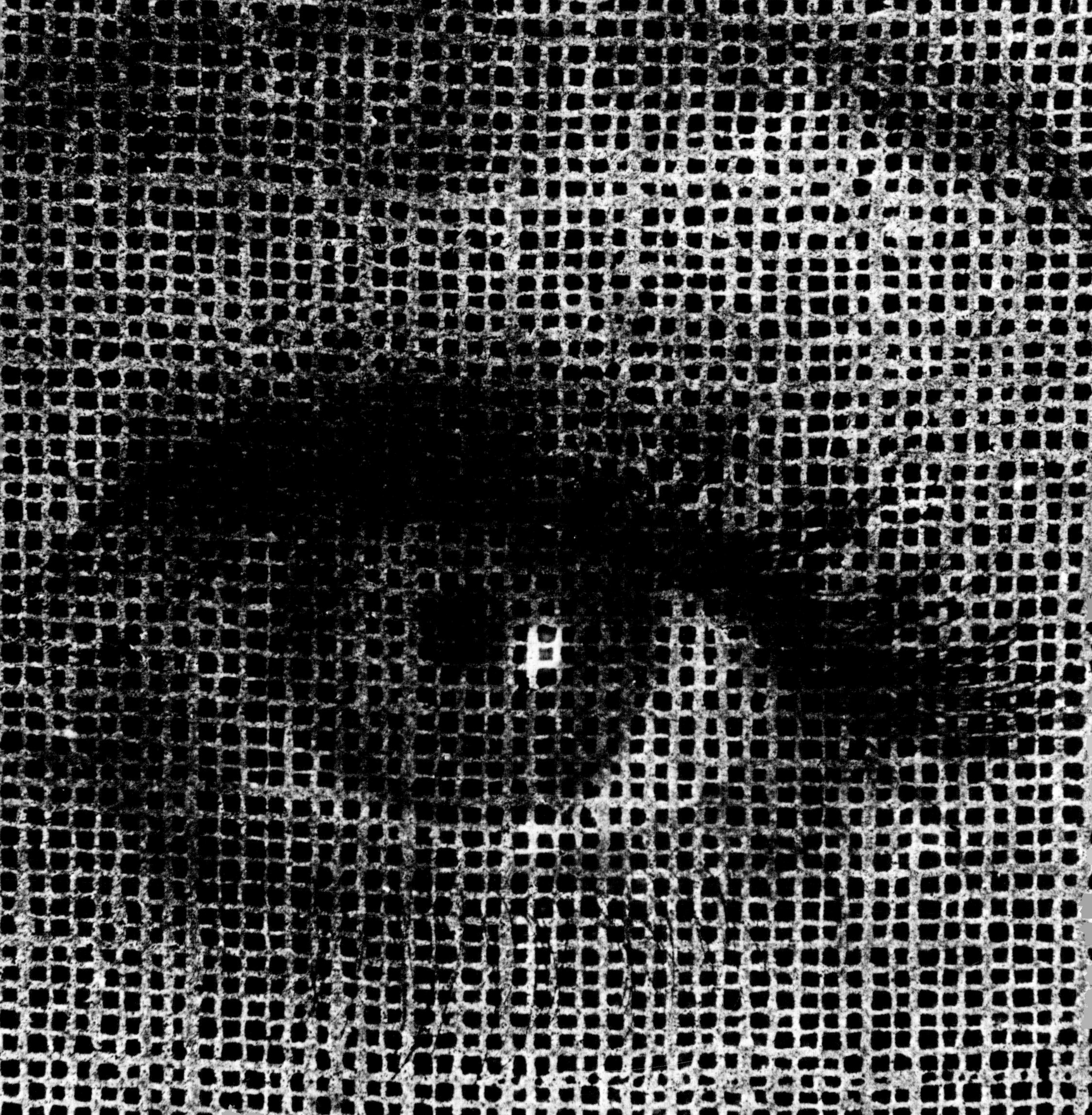

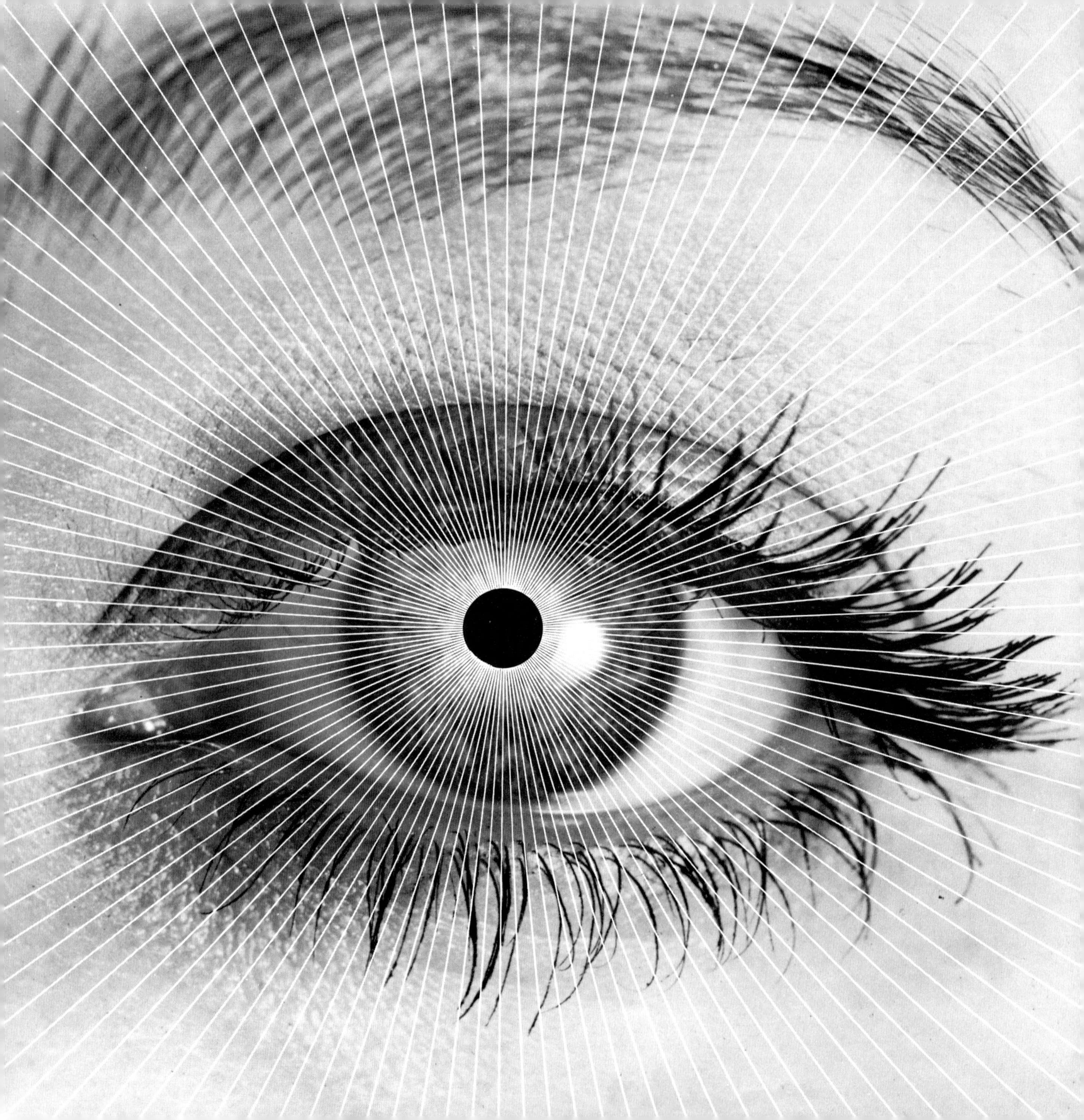

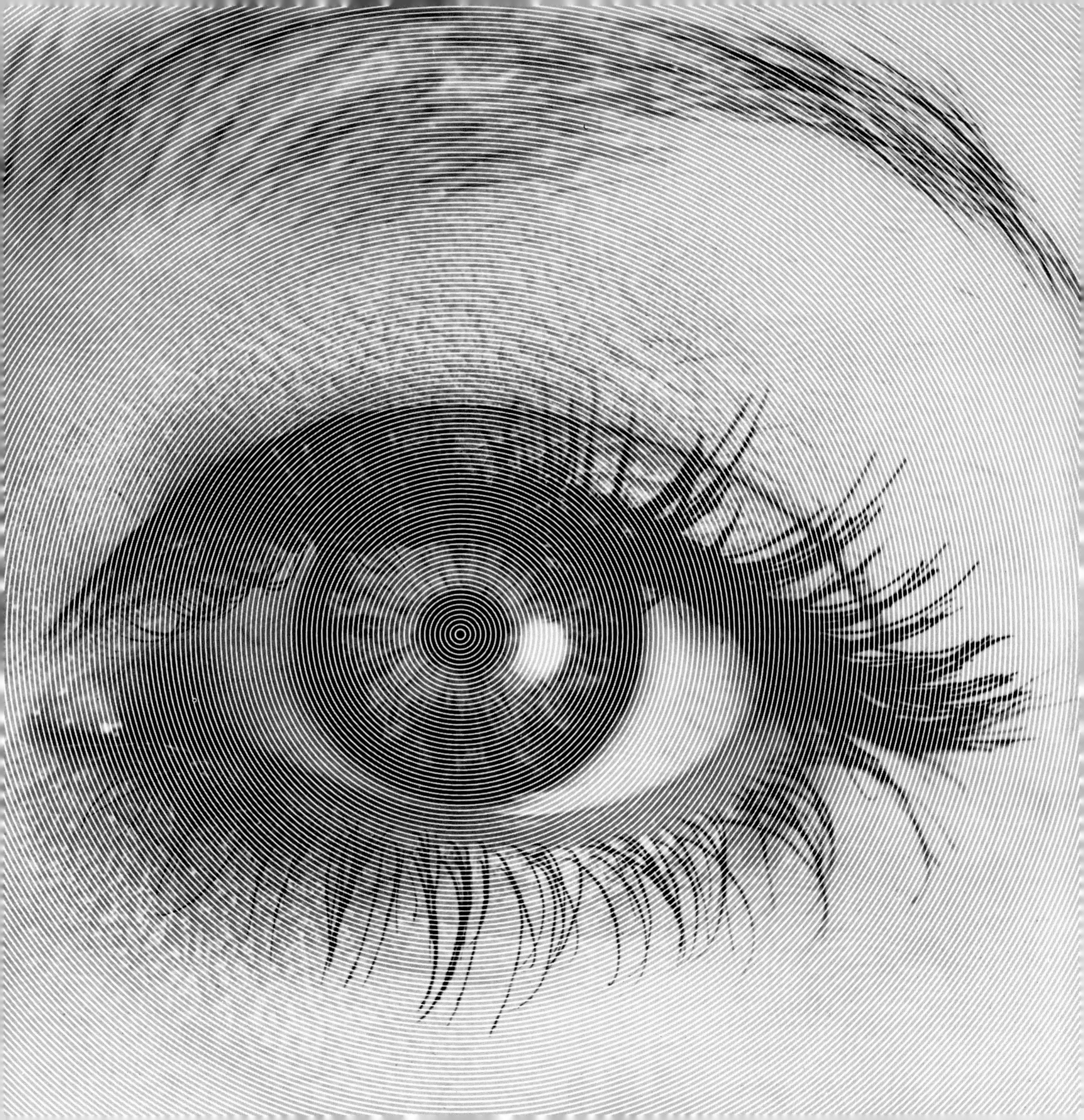

Screen Structures

Procedure

(1) Make negative from screen mask (foliage) (structure) onto film 1:1.

(2) Obtain positive by 1:1 (size to size) copying.

(3) Reversal from image (1:1), positive and negative onto film.

(4) Mount I: positive foliage structure and positive copy of image (in register with Mount II)

(5) Mount II: negative foliage structure and negative copy of image (in register with Mount II).

(6) Copy Mount I onto film 1:1. Result: negative eye structure on negative foliage structure.

(7) Copy Mount II onto film 1:1. Result: eye structure of positive foliage structure.

(8) Mount both results on top of each other in register and copy onto extra-hard paper.

(9) Result: see opposite page.

The example on the opposite page shows a further possible application of screen masks. The combination of negative and positive intermediate pictures alienates the contents of the picture into a total screen structure which maintains its proper symmetric form.

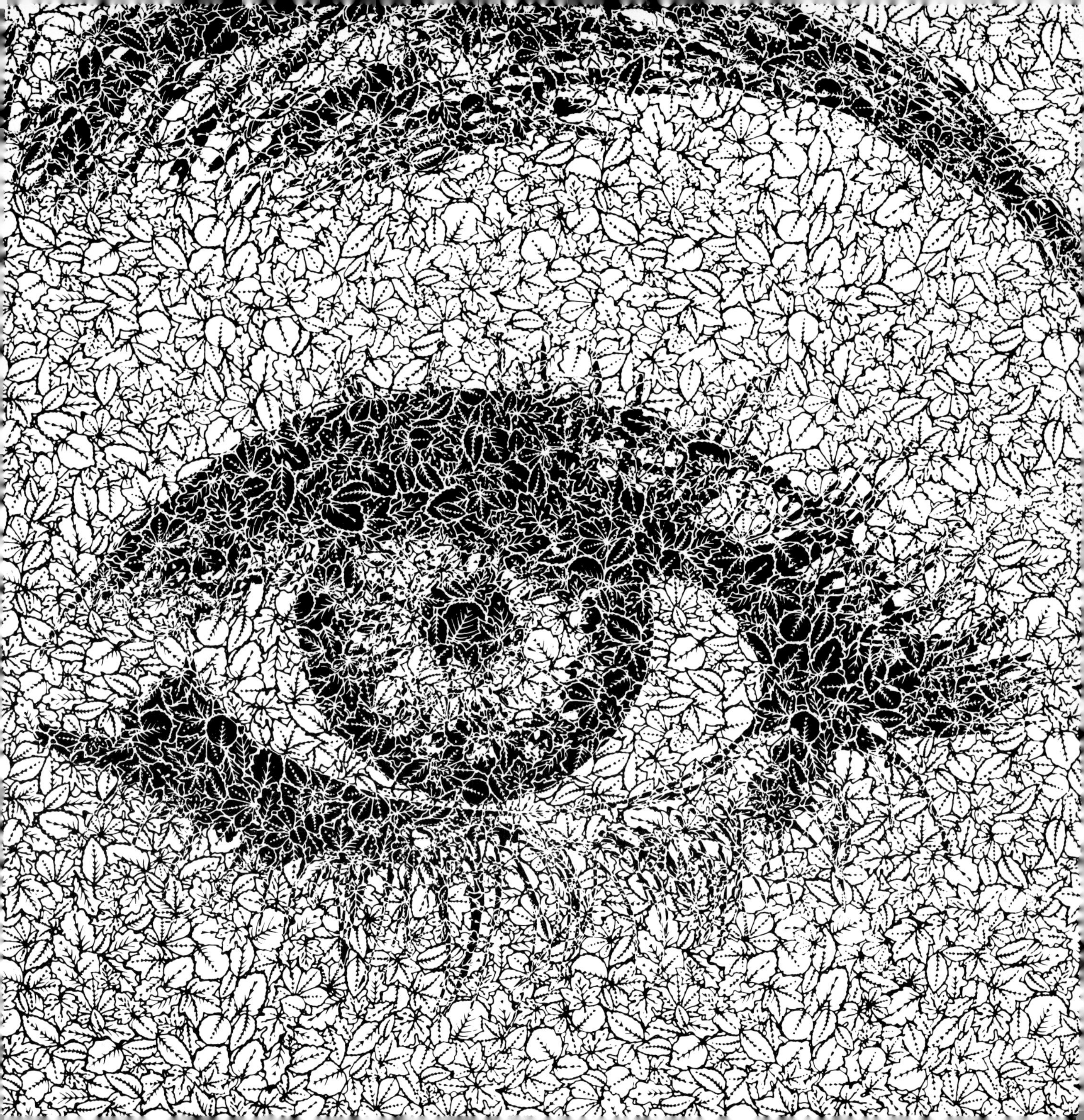

Three-Tone Screening

Procedure

(1) Glue registration markers on original negative.
(2) Make a positive in contact.
(3) From this, obtain 3 negatives of different density using different exposure times.
(4) Enlarge darkest negative onto photo paper.
(5) Mount middle tone negative in enlarger together with the transparent line screen (diagonally) and expose in register.
(6) Mount light negative in enlarger, with screen, lines going from right to left, and expose in register.
(7) Develop, stop, fix, wash, and dry.

With this procedure, a gray tone separation can be achieved with the help of a screen structure. From one positive, three differently exposed contrasty negatives are produced, showing different density ranges. These negatives are exposed in register one after the other onto print paper. The two lighter forms are combined line screens (diagonally opposed). During enlargement, different tonal values are achieved by partial superimposition of the lines.

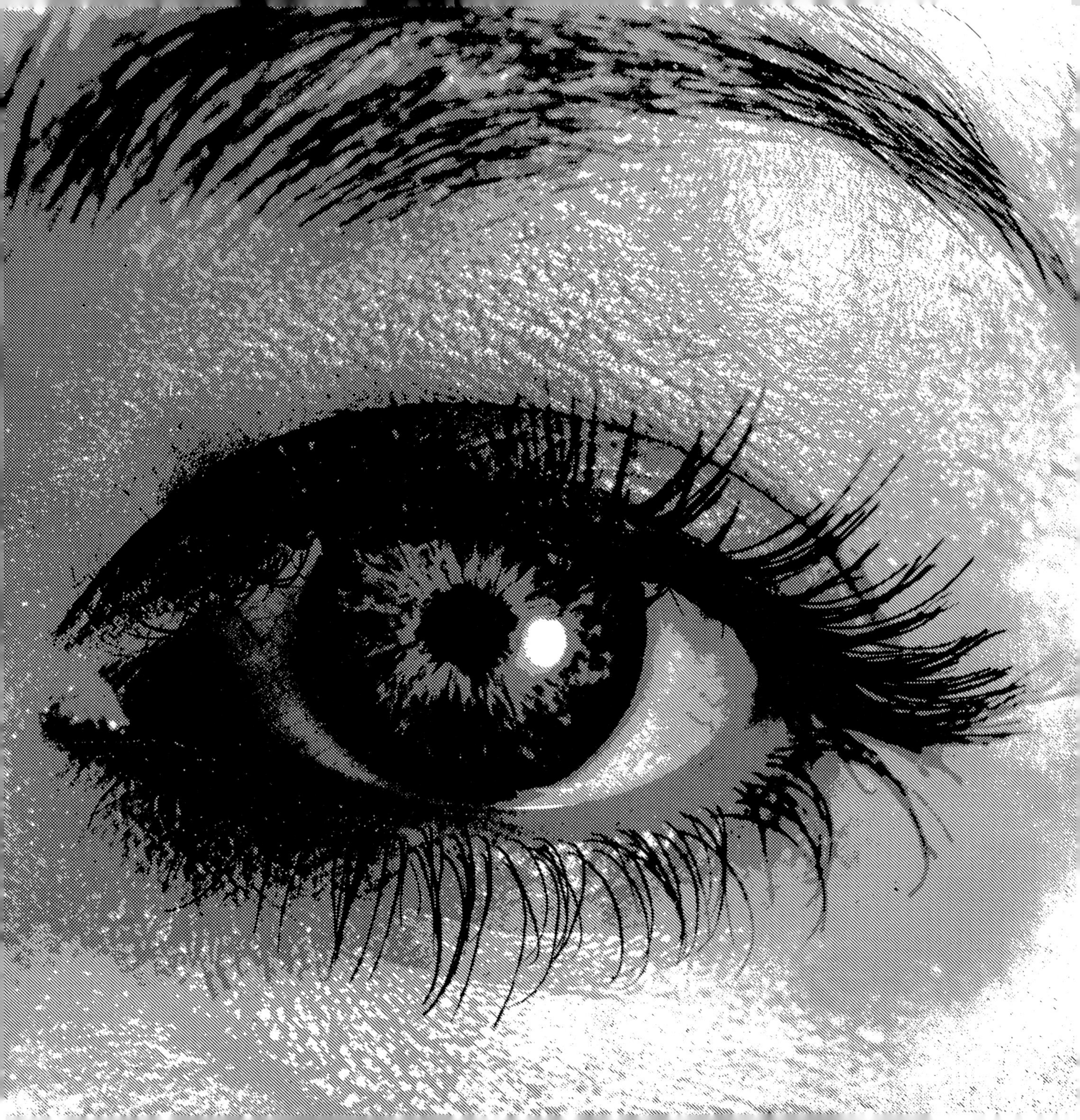

Screen Masks

Even a finished enlargement can still be changed with screen structures. The necessary adhesive or rubbing masks can be bought at graphic arts supply stores. The adjacent picture was prepared with an adhesive positive screen mask. The darker parts were obtained by consequently rubbing on of a second mask.

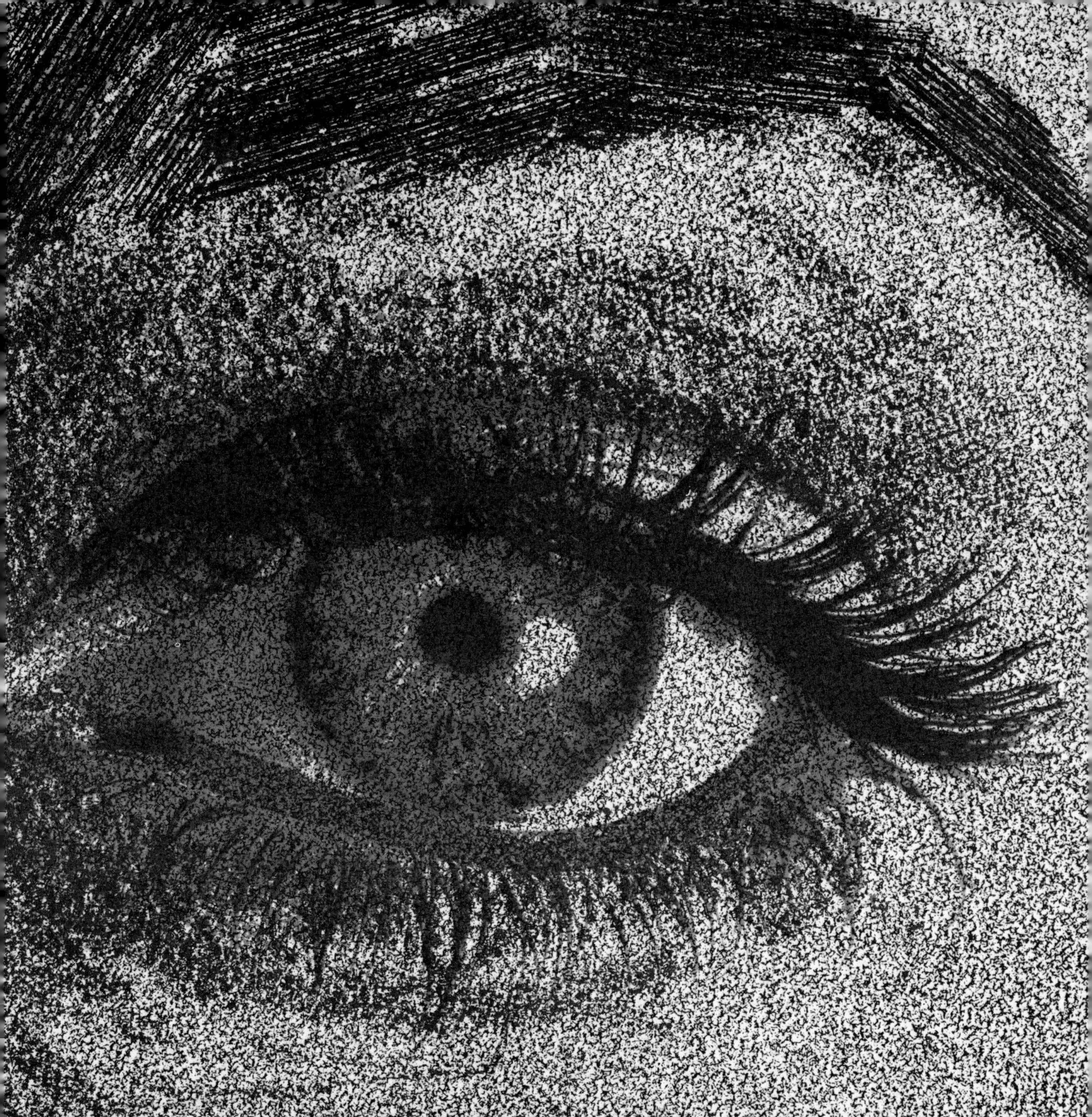

Distortions

Image distortions are most easily achieved by placing the easel at an angle or with partial deformation of the photographic paper. Another method is to place a curved glass object on the photo paper during exposition; similar results are obtained. In order to attain maximum sharpness, close the lens aperture as much as possible. It is not always easy to get satisfactory results. Professional laboratories may have the necessary equipment.

Page 61: Distortion by using a warped board.
Page 62: Thirty-six percent stretching of the image with a distortion lens.
Page 63: Globe modification, by using a glass half sphere and placing it on the negative during exposure.

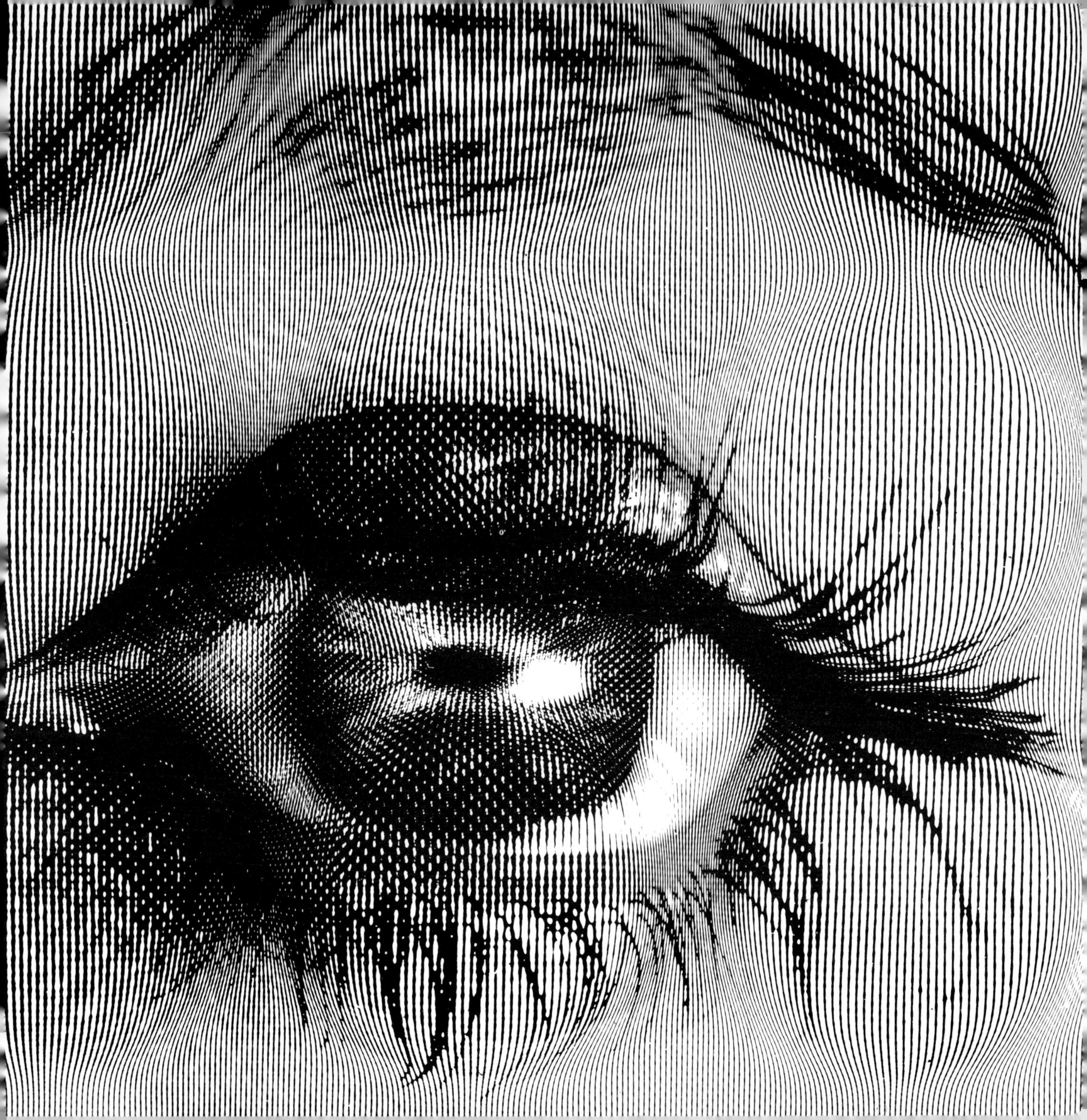

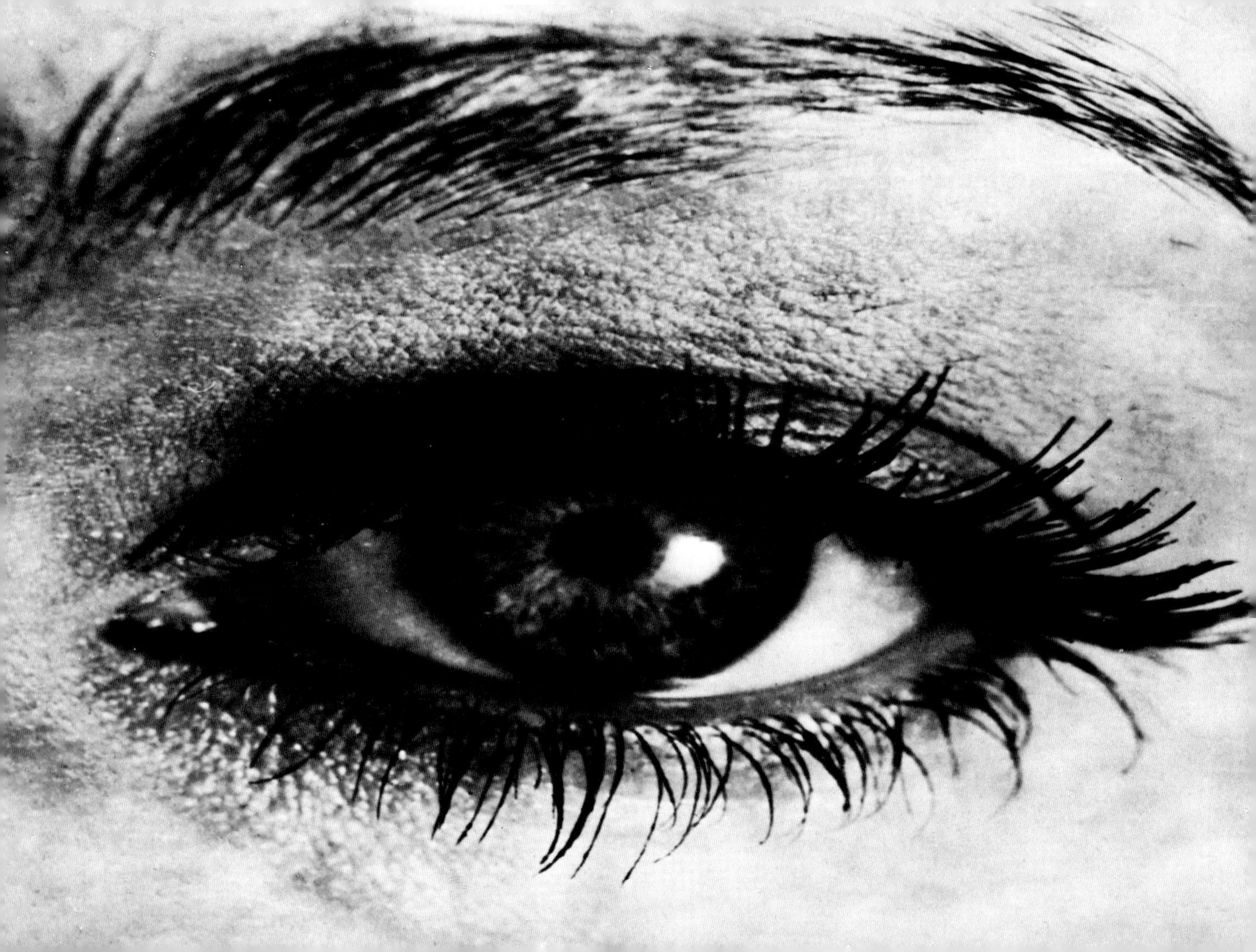

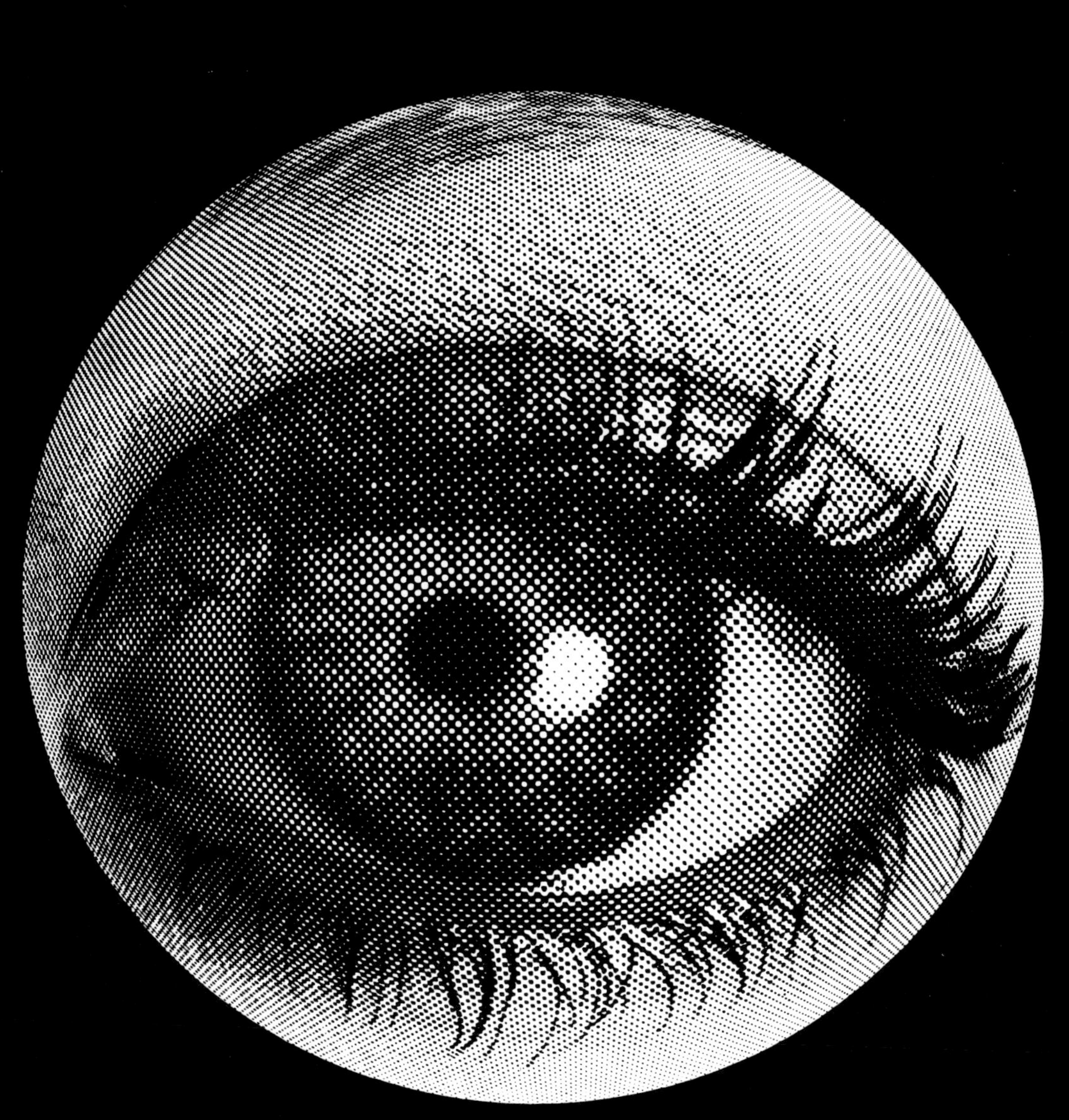

Superimposition

Superimposing into an already exposed image can serve to enhance or to alter the image content. The technique is as follows: before enlarging, one covers the portion of the negative into which superimposition is desired. The remainder of the photographic paper is marked. Into this section, the other image motif will be exposed, filling the space if possible.

Procedure

(1) Cover the parts to be left free on the negative.
(2) Put in enlarger, determine image area, and mark free areas. Expose.
(3) Prepare second negative to fit the free areas and expose into blank field.
(4) Develop, stop, fix, wash, and dry.

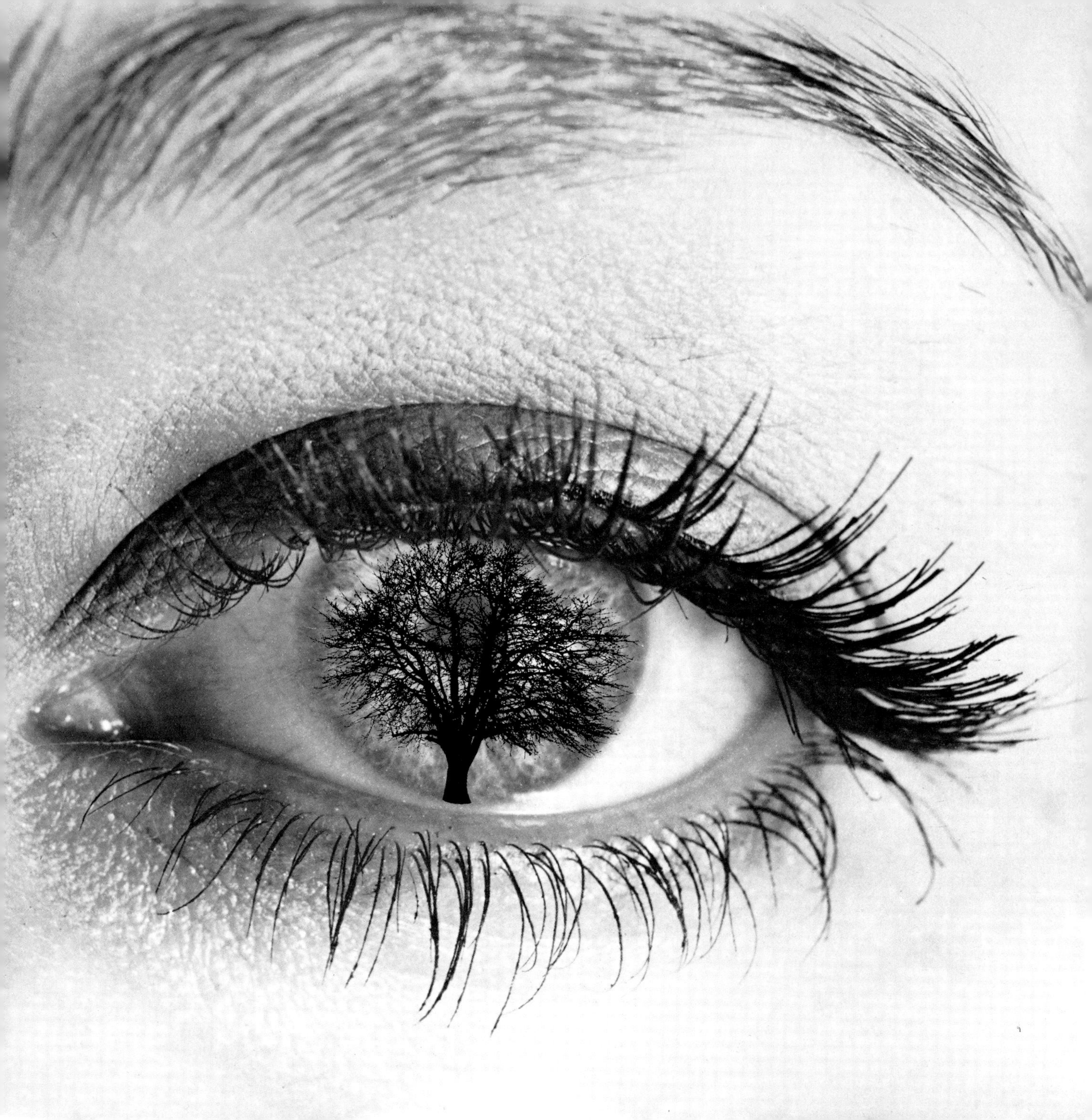

COLOR TONING

Toning

In photochemistry, a profusion of toning processes are known which render the image into a desirable monochromatic color tone. The scale of colors extends from sepia hues to intensely saturated colors.

In these procedures, the black silver is normally dissolved from the paper permanently and is replaced by the desired color tone. The background remains white.

In the adjacent example, Tetenal Multitoner was used. Depending upon the procedure, it is advisable to use the manufacturer's directions.

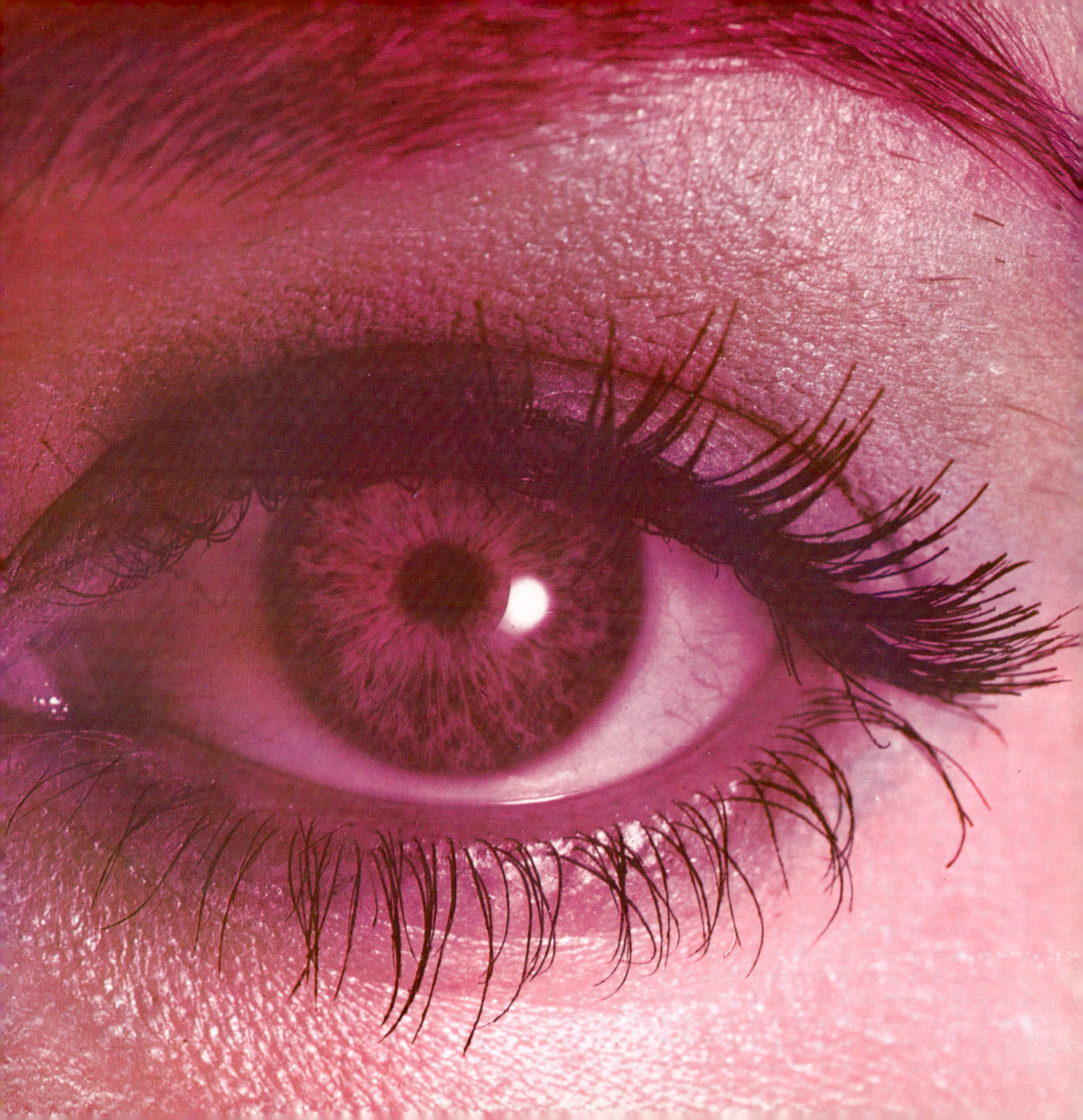

Albumin Glazing Dyes

Procedure

(1) Rinse the picture with water.
(2) Place the wet picture onto a glass plate, emulsion up and wipe flat.
(3) Prepare glazing dyes in small bowls.
(4) Apply dyes to photo with a large brush or cotton swab (use diluted dyes and brush on several times to avoid color spots).

Often, albumin glazing dyes are used to tone or dye matte or glossy black-and-white enlargements. These dyes are transparent and can easily be mixed with each other. When using these dyes, separate areas can be colored individually. The whole image can also be dyed to the extent that the result has no resemblance to a conventional color enlargement. In the example, a black-and-white repetitive copy was thus treated.

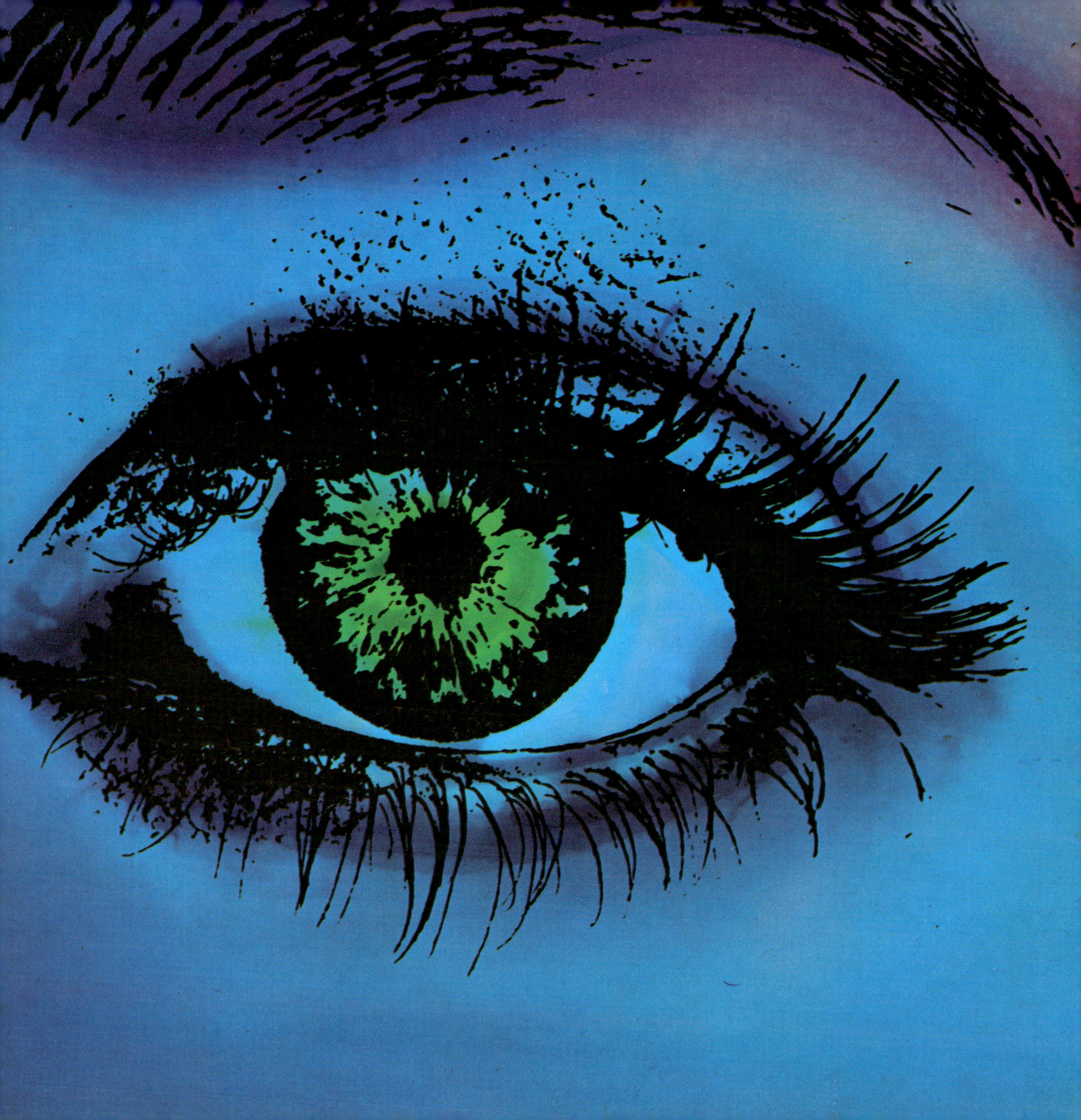

Toning and Albumin Glazing Dyes

Procedure

(1) Tone black-and-white image (see procedure on pg. 64).
(2) Then rinse and wipe onto glass plate.
(3) Apply glazing dye with brush or cotton swab partially onto the wet picture and spread.

A combination of toning and albumin glazing dyes offers increased possibilities of coloring.

In the example shown, a black-and-white image was toned with Tetenal Multitoner and partially colored with three different albumin dyes.

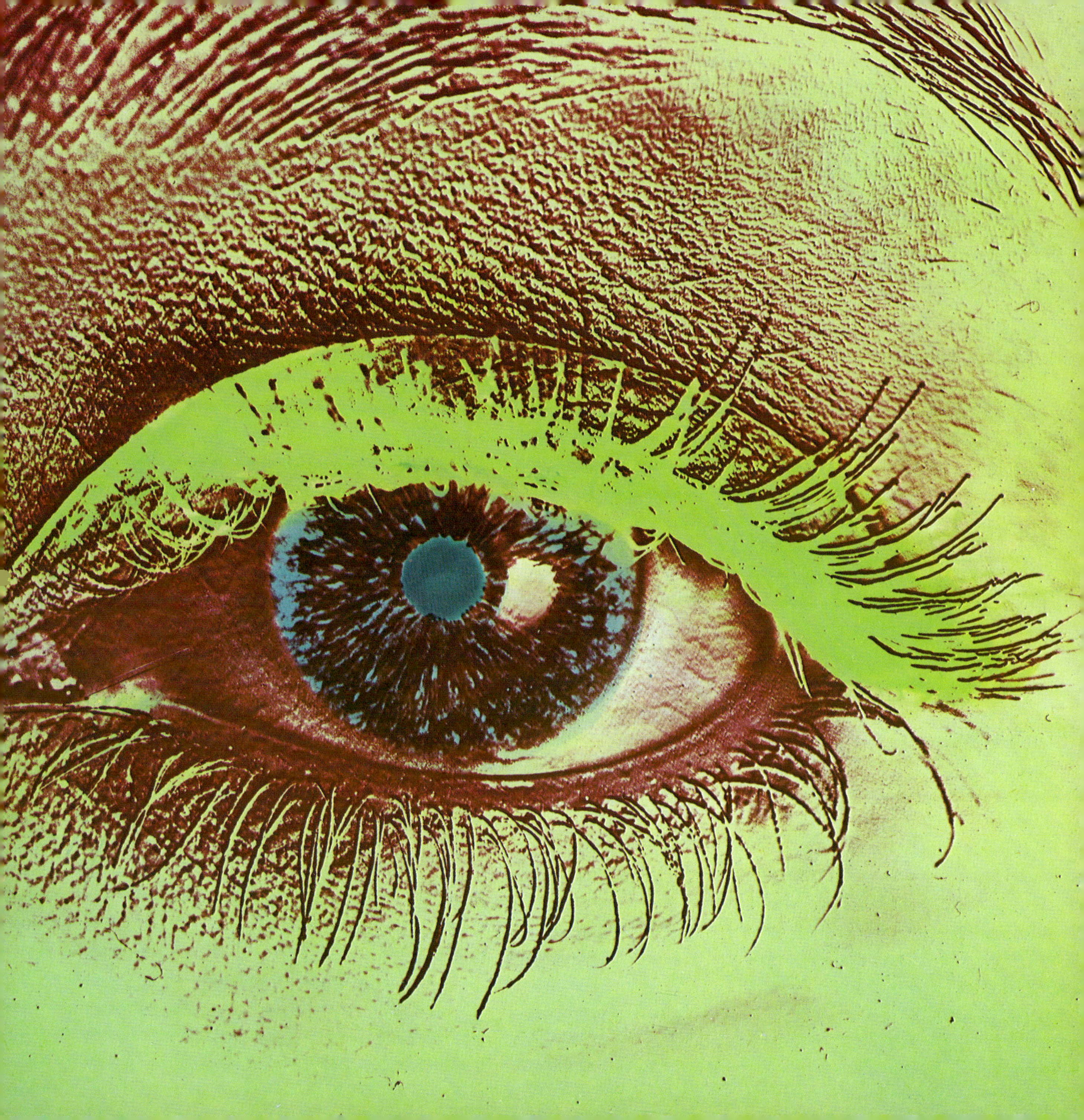

Felt-Tip Penning

Felt tip pens are available in a large selection of hues for effective coloring of a black-and-white enlargement. The luminosity and intensity of these colors can be used for unusual brilliance and expression.

Page 75: Felt pen colors were smeared onto the picture and subsequently dissolved with a gasoline-soaked brush.

Page 76: The superimposed mounting of two different photographic techniques was partially colored with felt tip pens.

Page 77: The white line structure of a negative solarization was painted out with different colors.

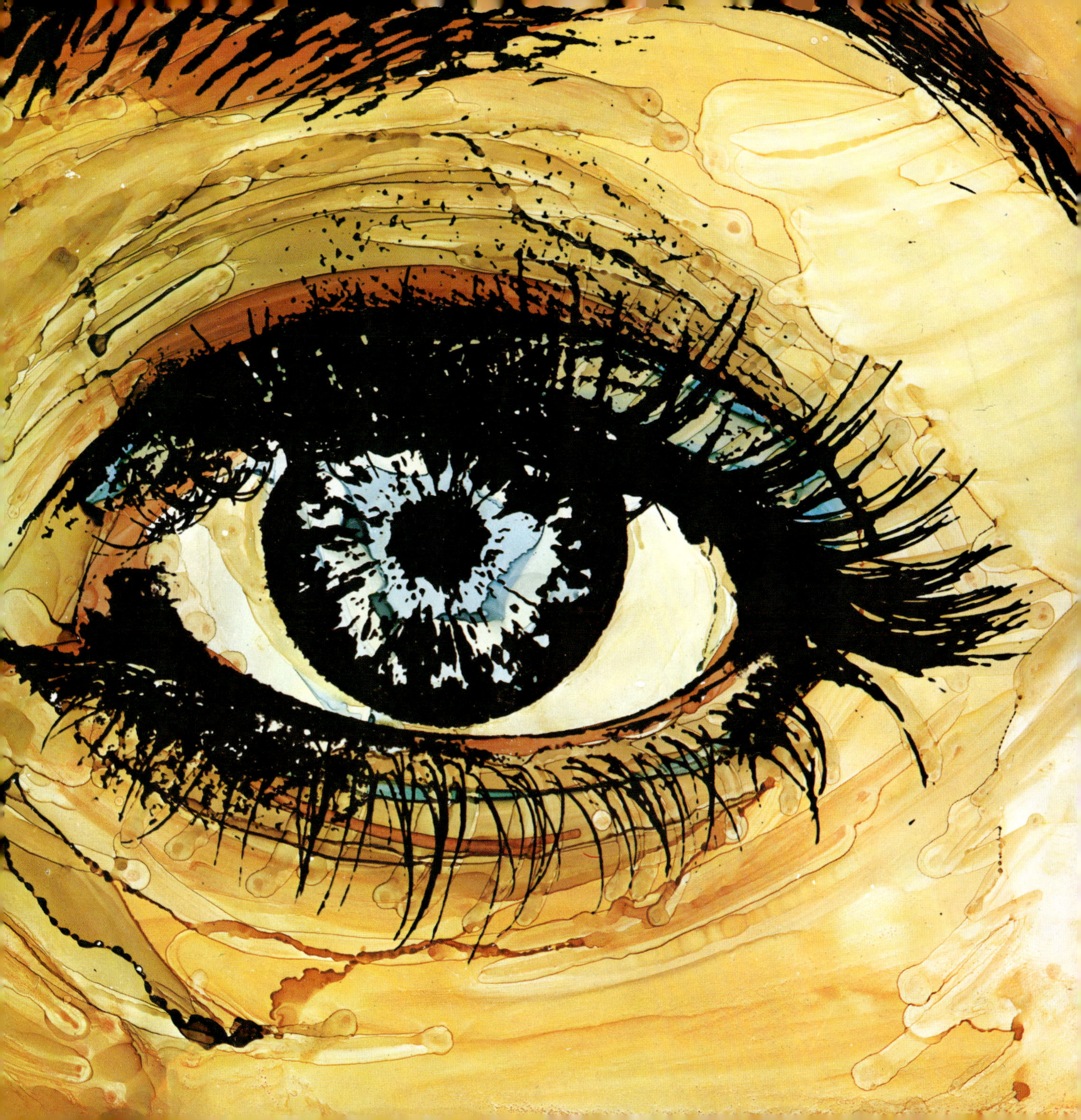

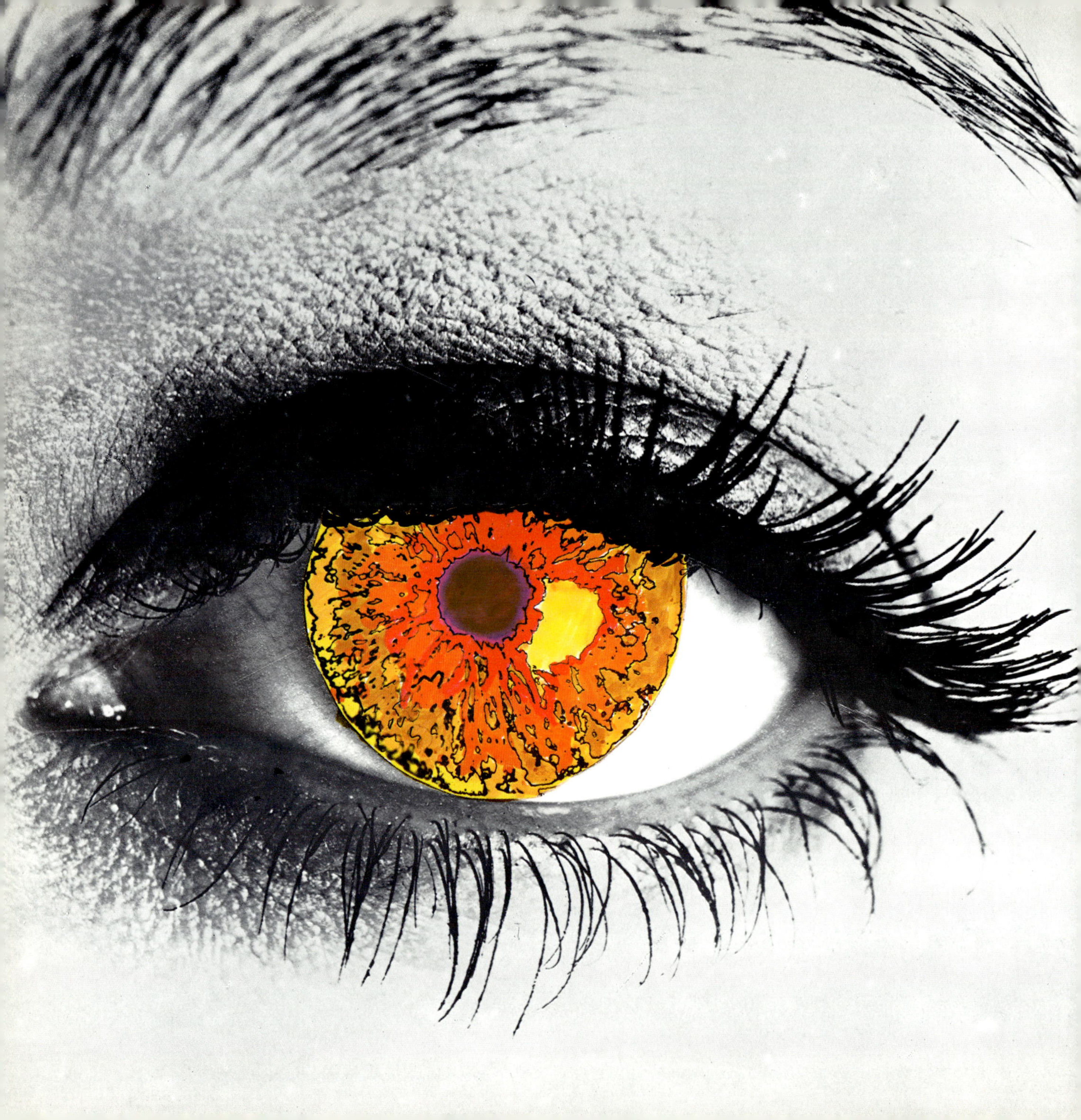

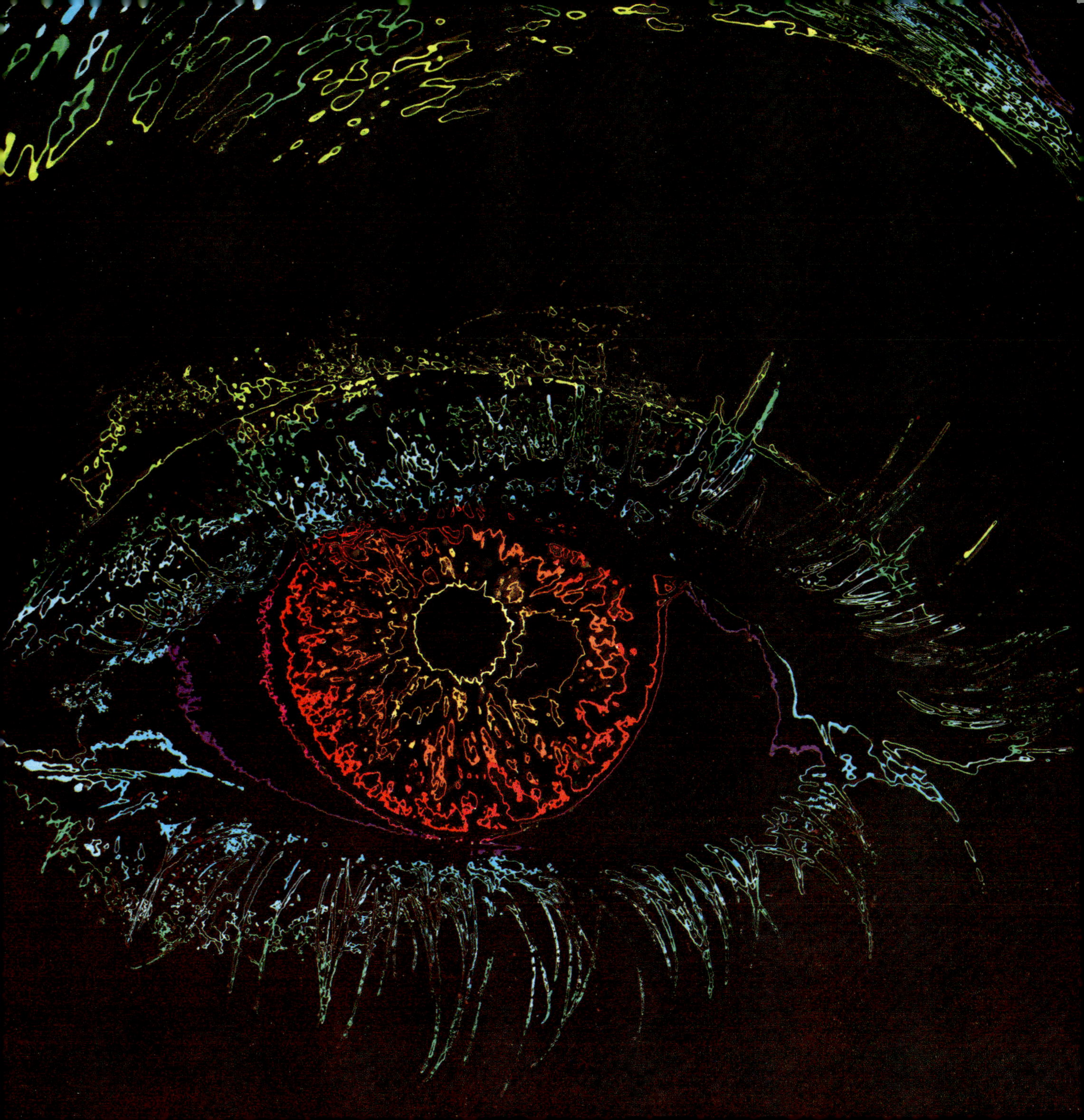

Spray Technique

Procedure

(1) Mount black-and-white enlargement on cardboard.
(2) Cover areas which shouldn't be colored with stencil. Spray desired aerosol color evenly on uncovered areas at a 3 to 4 inch distance (ca. 10 cm).
(3) Allow to dry.
(4) Remove stencil. Cover areas and spray with next color.
(5) Repeat until desired effect is achieved.

The spray technique is done with a spray gun which disperses the albumin glazing dyes and retouching colors into a fine aerosol-type mist with compressed air. Clean and transition-free hues can thus be obtained. If sharply defined contours are desired, stencils can be used which are made of transparent cellophane or plastic.

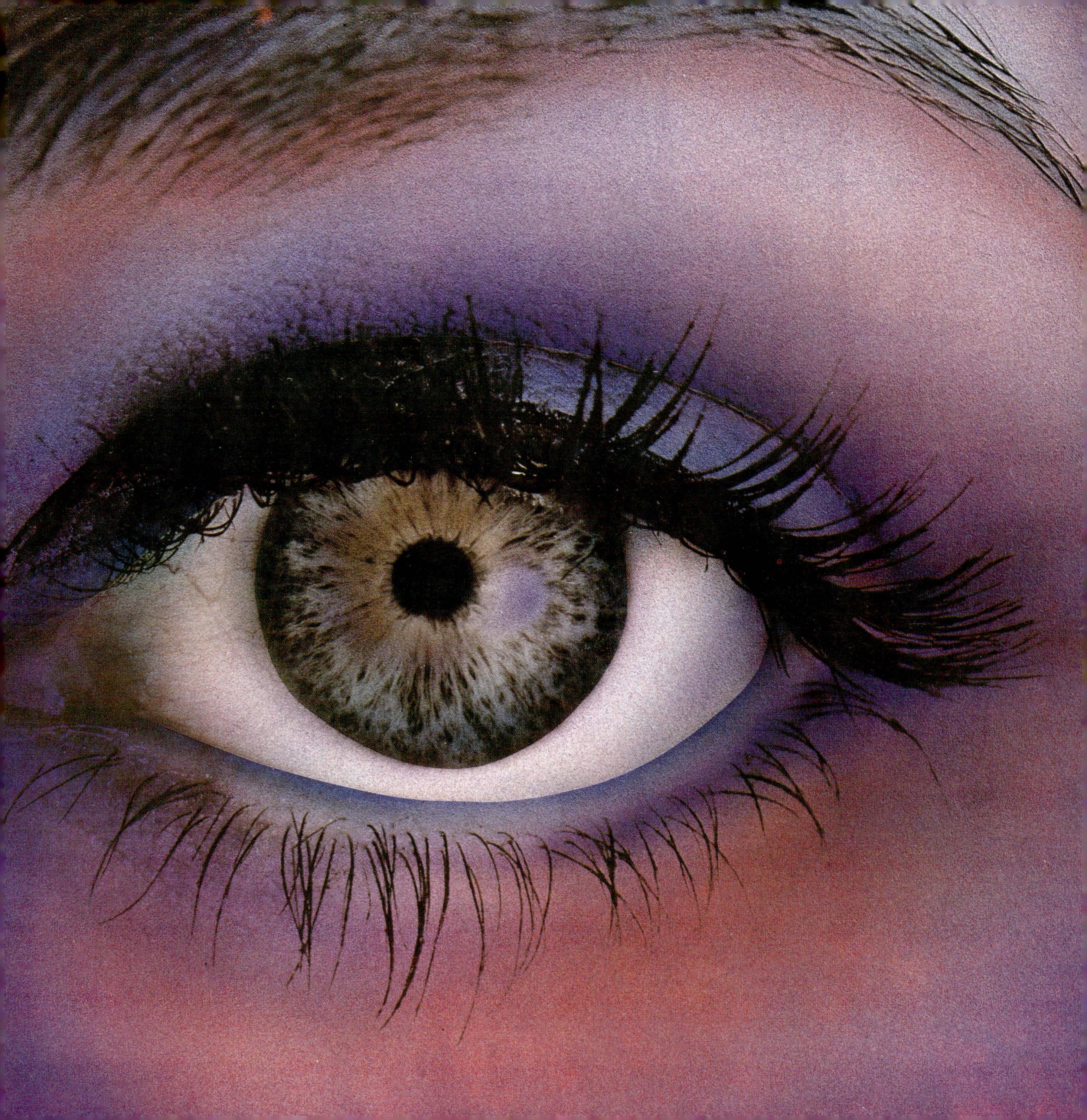

Colored Masks

Procedure

(1) Remove backing from mask.
(2) Press or rub onto desired areas.
(3) With a respective knife cut out desired shapes of mask. With a smooth object, rub these masks on.

Adhesive transparent or opaque masks can be used to add color to black-and-white photos easily and cleanly. A further possibility is offered when using rub-on masks which can be rubbed onto the enlargement with a smooth flat tool. Color masks are available in art stores in different color tones.

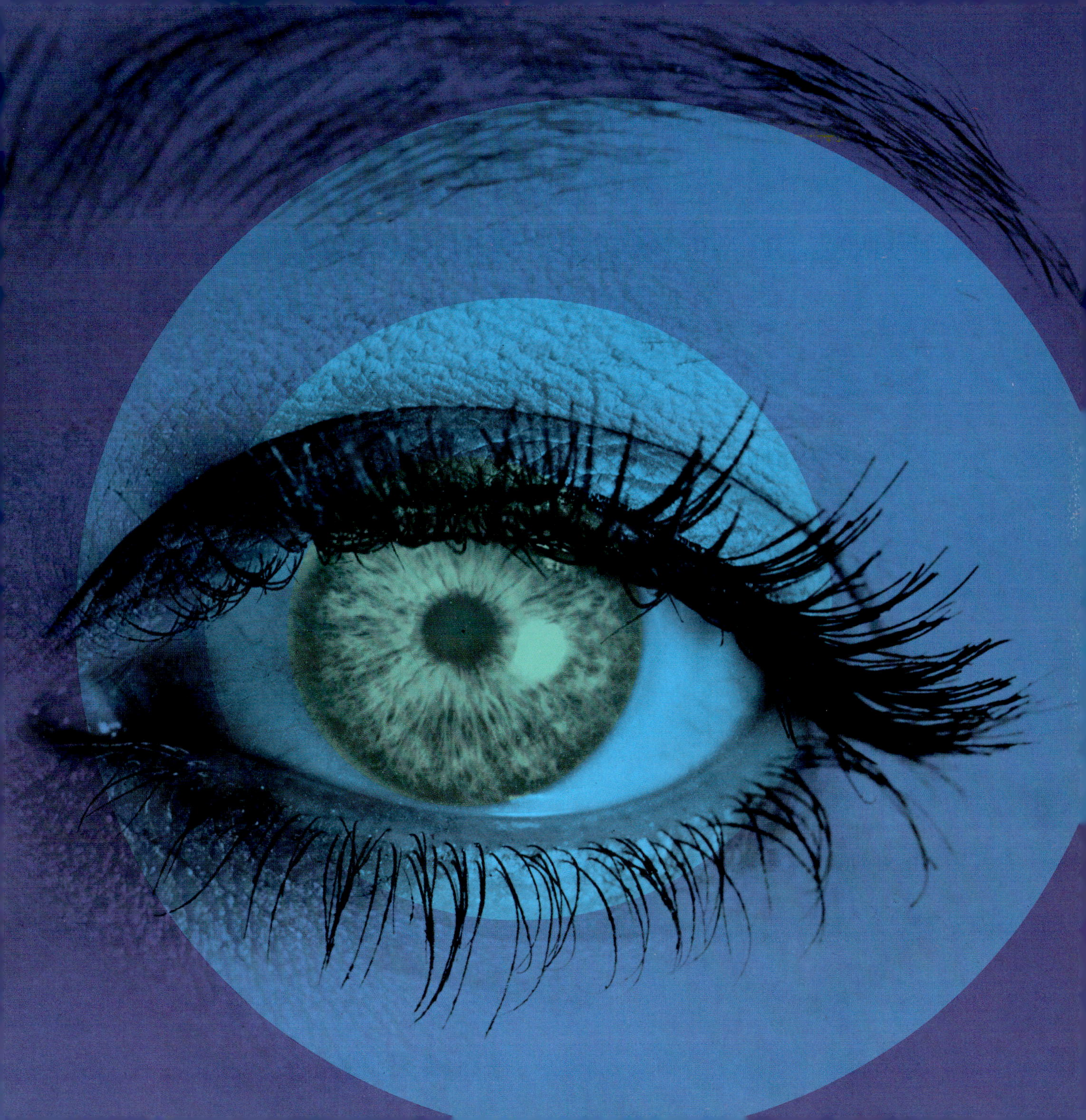

COLOR-KEY

Color-Key

Color-Key is a polyester film with an UV light-sensitive, transparent or opaque color coating. On these colorful masks, one can copy any contrasty transparency under daylight conditions. The only necessary accessories are an UV light source and developing liquids. There are many shades of Color-Key film available. The advantage of this masking technique is that you can obtain a high-contrast transparency of the image in a short time.

By mounting various color masks, one can accomplish an indefinite number of color combinations and mixtures. The mounted masks can be used directly as printable images for plate etchings. To obtain a color paper copy, one has only to make an enlargement using a color process.

Page 85: Negative multiple copies of varying density.
Page 86: Composition with 2 different colors.
Page 87: Combination of multiple copies and solarization.
Page 87: A colored copy on different color background.
Page 88: Mount of 3 objects in different sizes and colors superimposed.

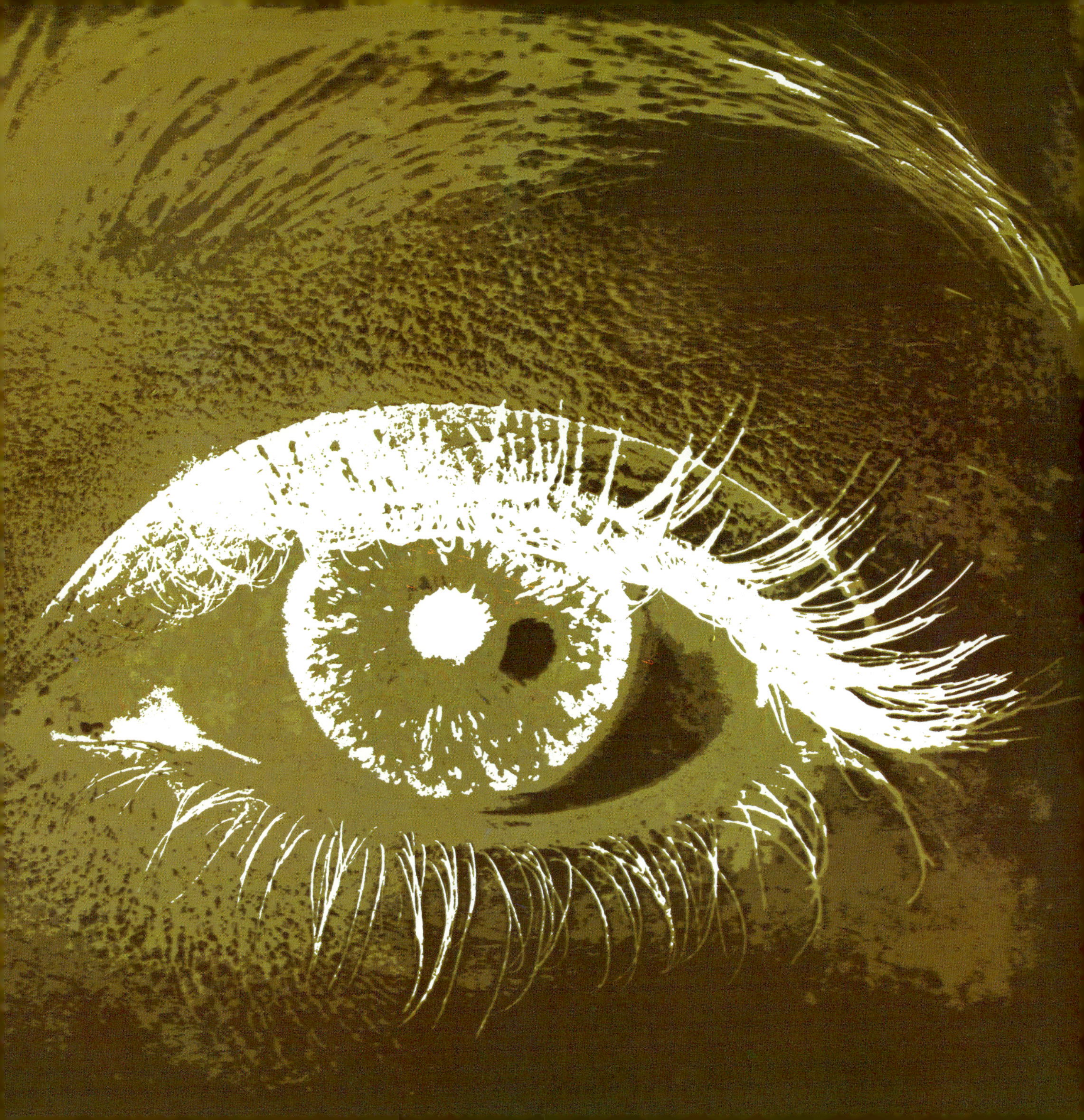

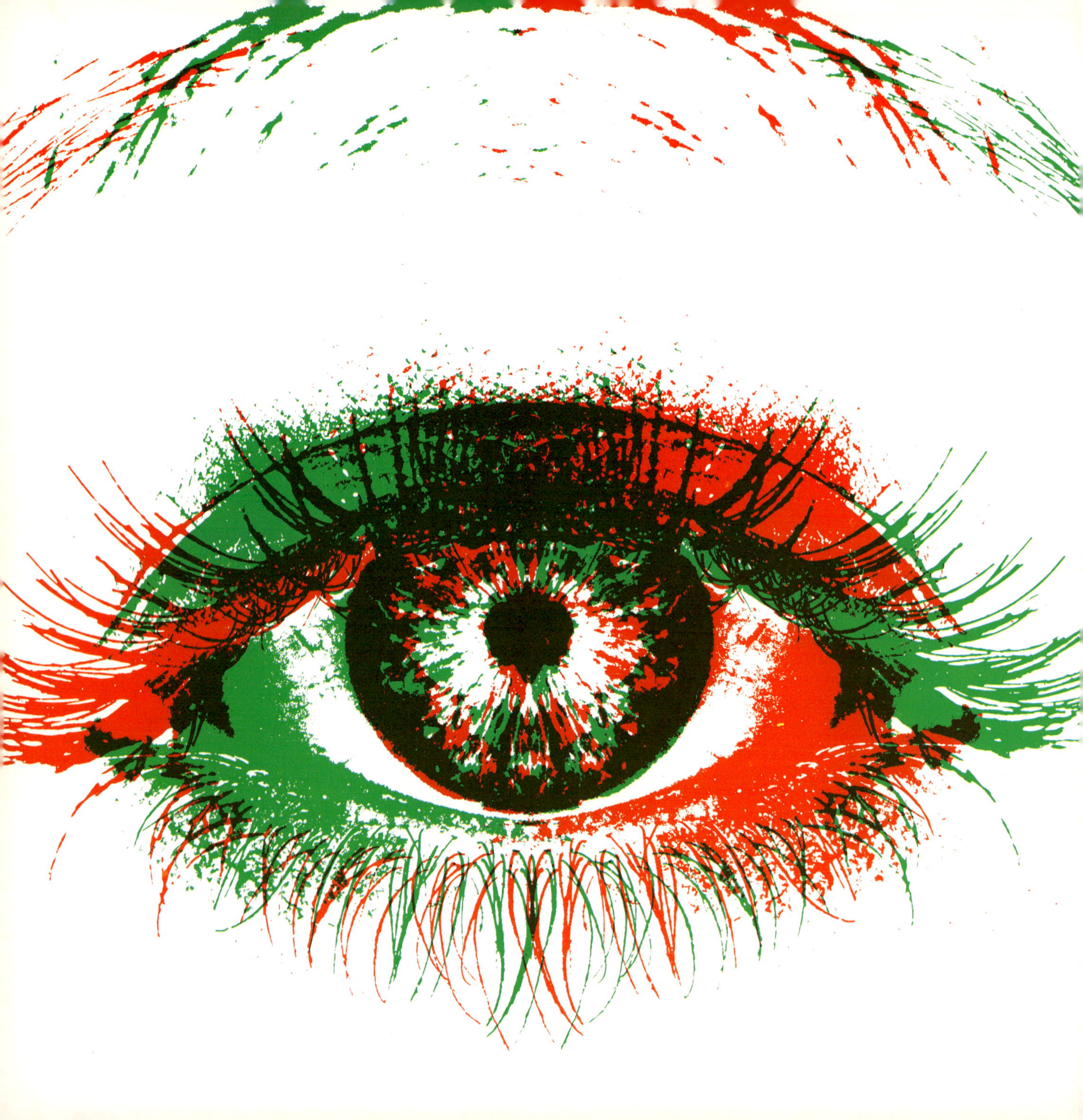

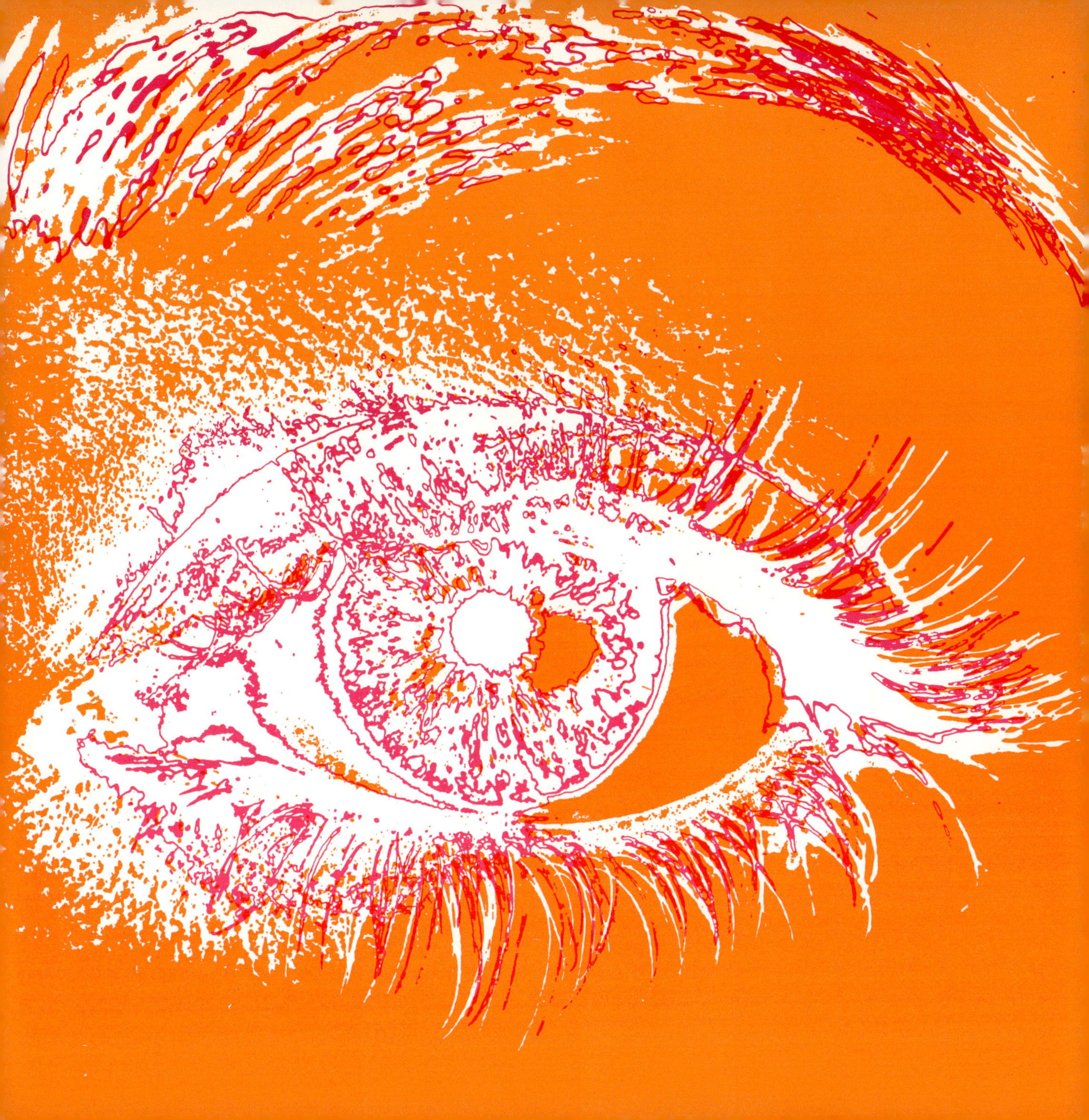

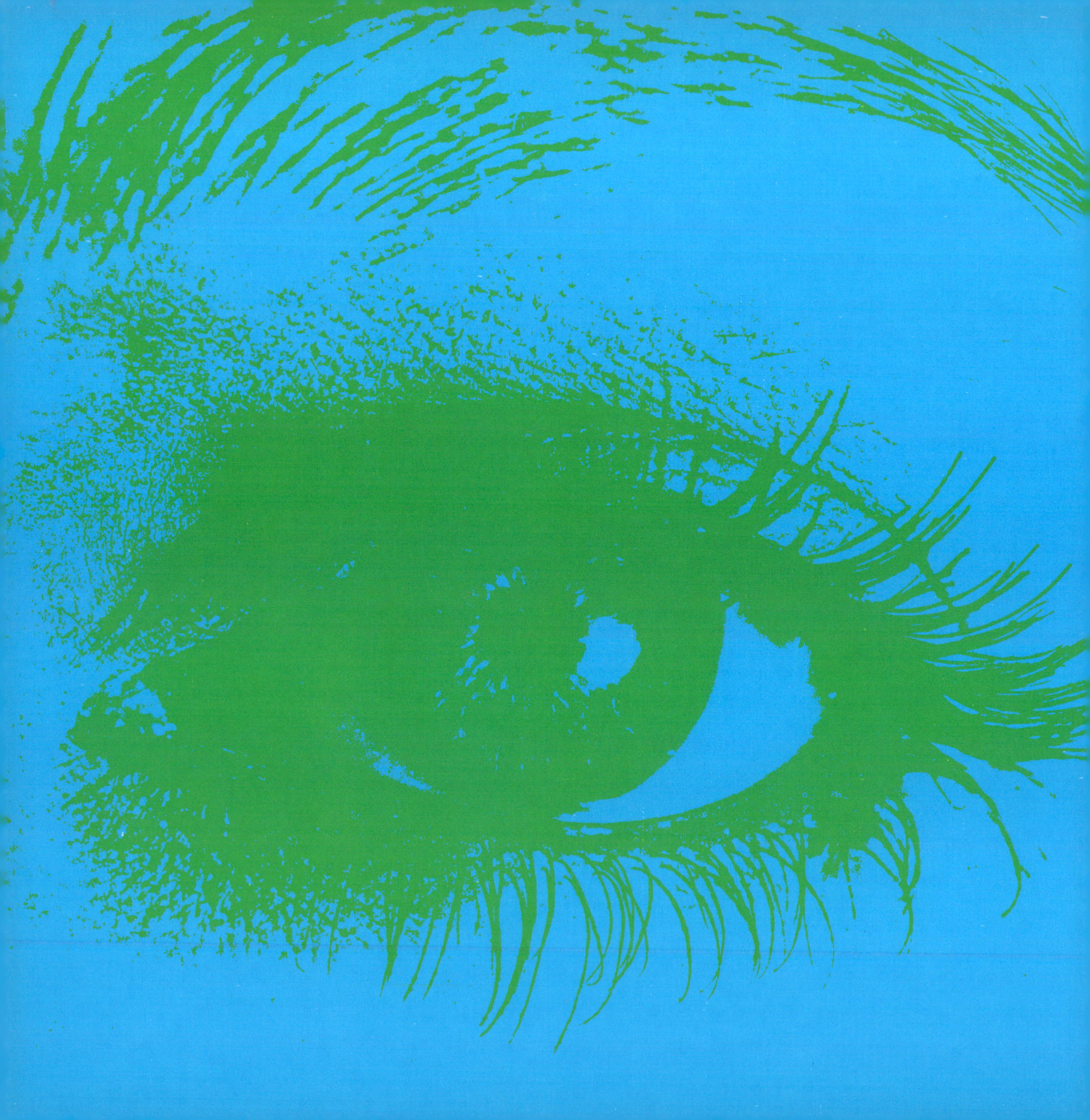

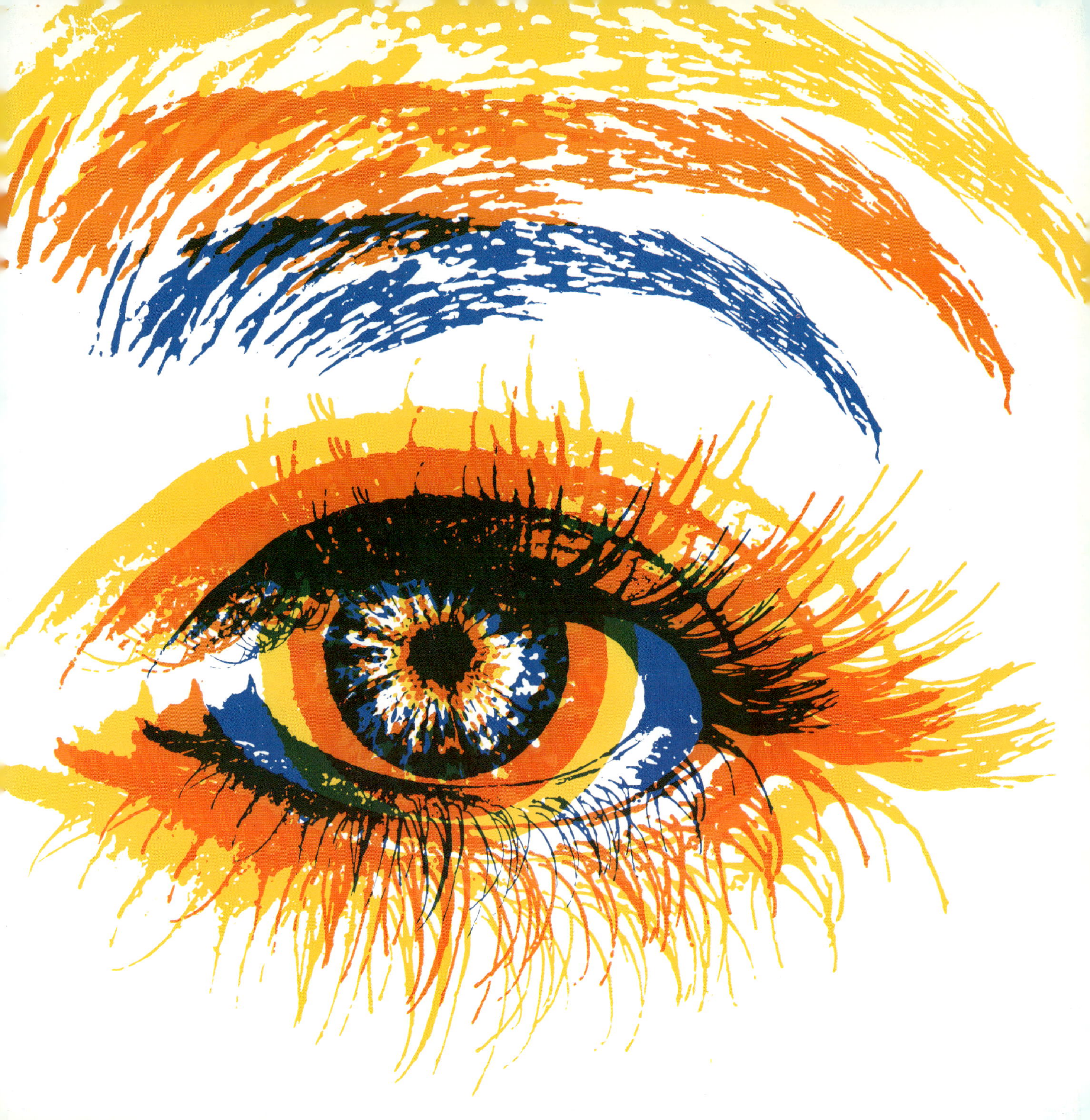

Tone Separation With Color-Key

Similar to black-and-white or color tone separations, differently dense negatives and positives are copied from the original negative. From the desired negatives and positives, transparent and differently colored Color-Keys can be made and mounted in register. When superimposing several color masks, the lighter colors should be placed under the darker ones.

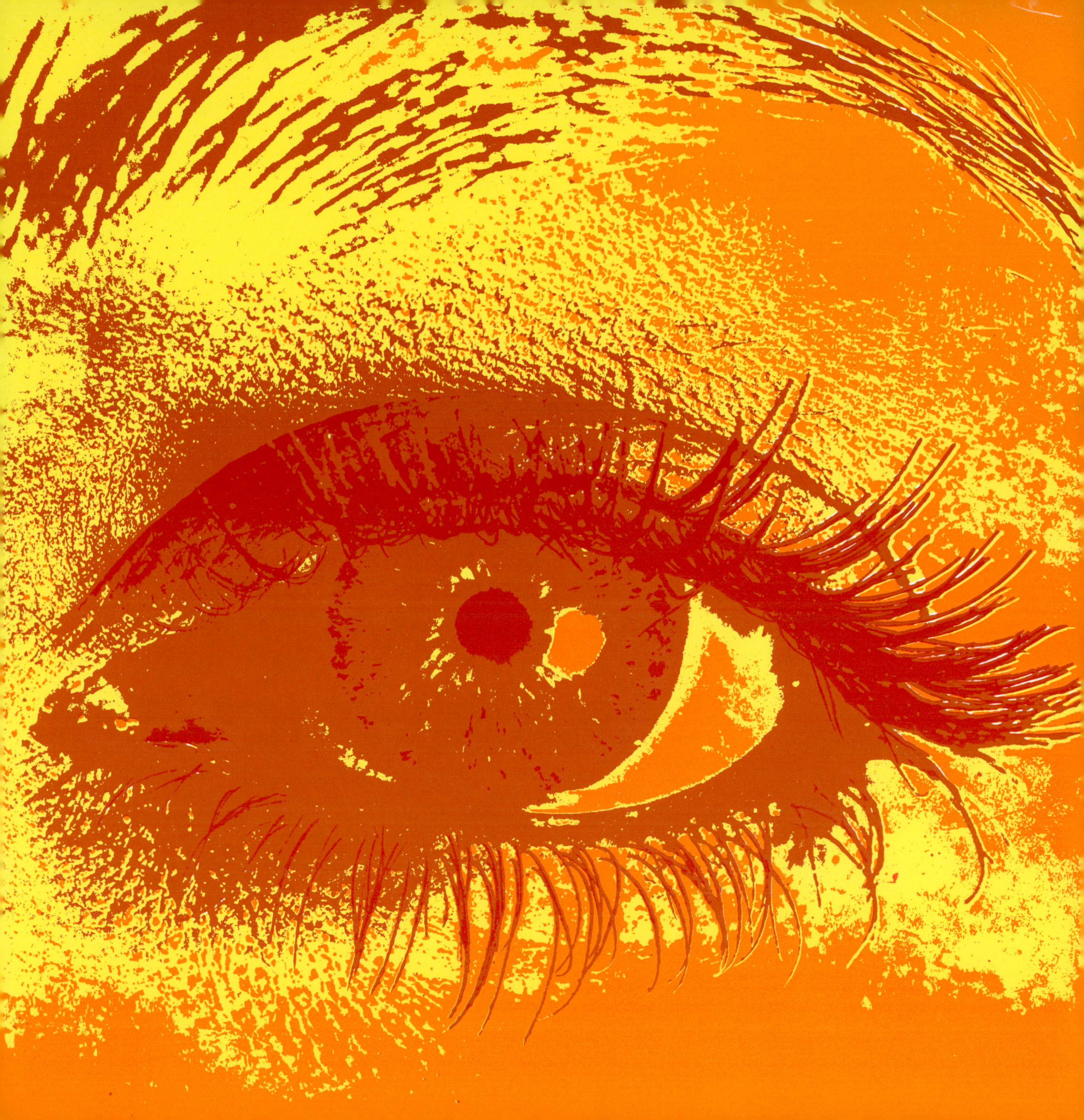

COLOR LAB TECHNIQUES

Enlargement of Color Negative Film

Procedure

(1) Place color negative film in enlarger.
(2) Determine exposure time with densitometer.
(3) Expose with white light to determine filtration.
(4) Color develop.
(5) Judge results and correct colorcast, depending on hue and intensity.
(6) Expose again; follow the manufacturer's processing recommendations.

A color enlargement is made from a color negative (usually masked) and colored in complementary colors. Depending upon the photograph's light source, the enlarger light source, and differences in film emulsion, a subtractive or additive color-correcting filtration has to be made. Then, the color developing processes are done according to the manufacturer's recommendations.

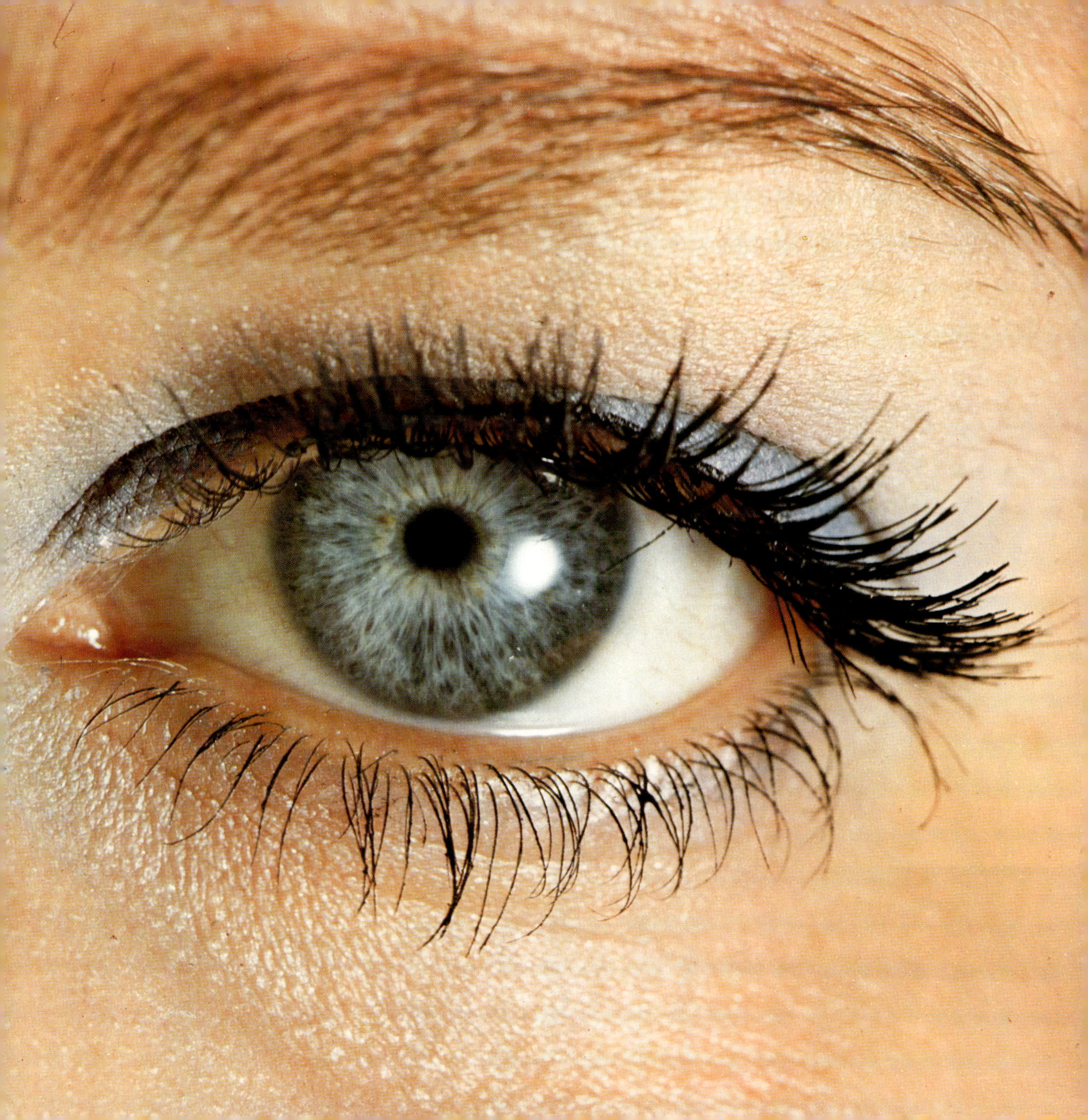

False-Color Enlargements

By overfiltering in any one of the given color hues, certain intentional color shifts can be achieved with the help of high color filter densities. Such manipulated results render additional effects and stimulation to an original.

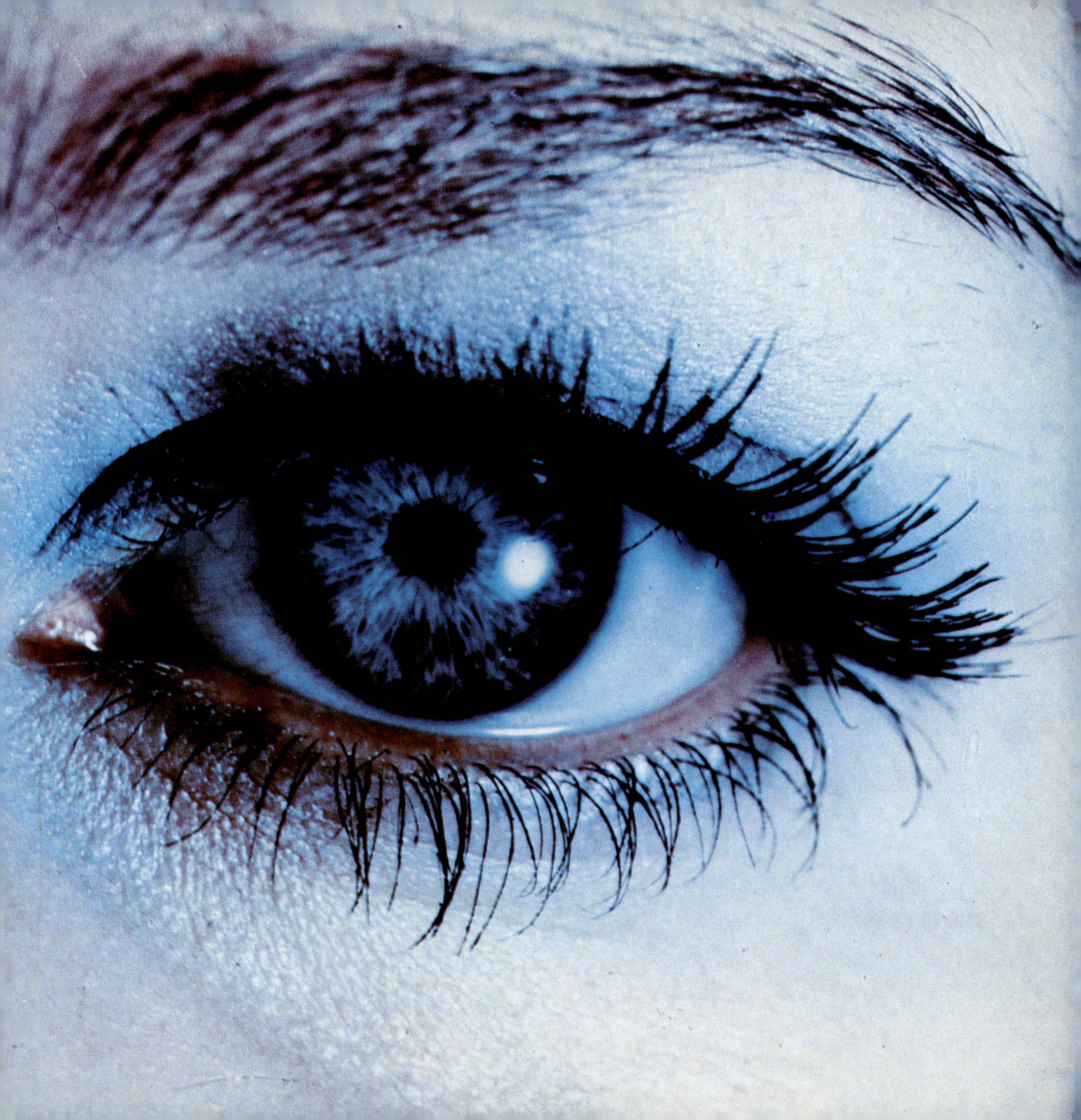

Color-Slide Enlargements

If a color slide instead of a color negative is enlarged, a negative enlargement in complementary colors is obtained.

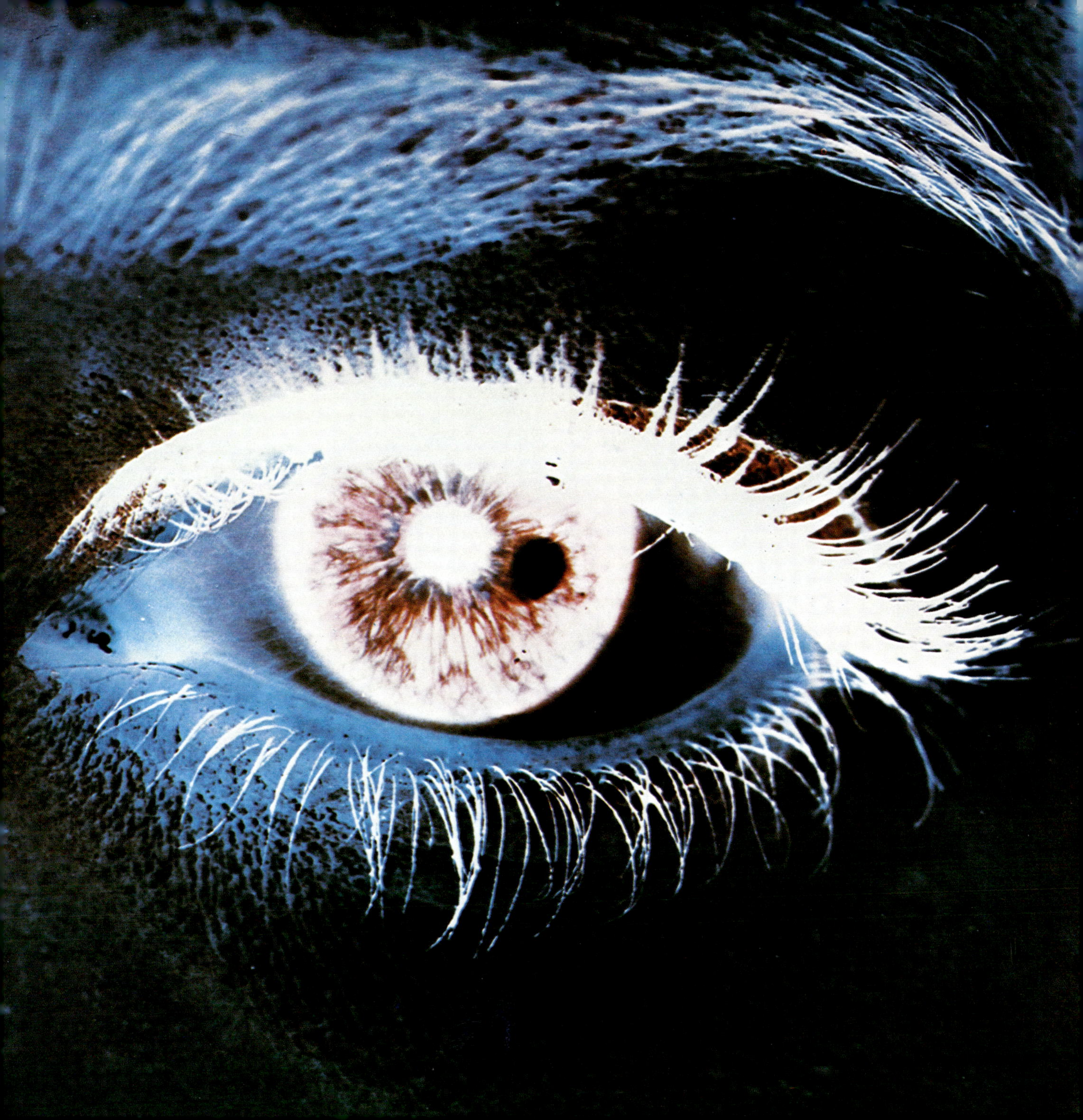

Color-Tone Separation

Procedure

(1) *Registration markers are glued onto a black-and-white or color negative.*

(2) *With differently adjusted exposures, copy five to six positives on high-contrast film copying material, thus producing different densities.*

(3) *Obtain contrasty negatives with similar exposure times.*

(4) *Expose about four fitting forms (negative or positive) in sequence and in register with individually selected color hues onto color paper.*

(5) *Follow the manufacturer's processing recommendations.*

Colored and black-and-white tone separations are obtained by similar technical means. Instead of gray or black values, one obtains different color values or steps. They can be composed in the same color tone or in mixed color hues. Every intermediate negative is assigned a desired color.

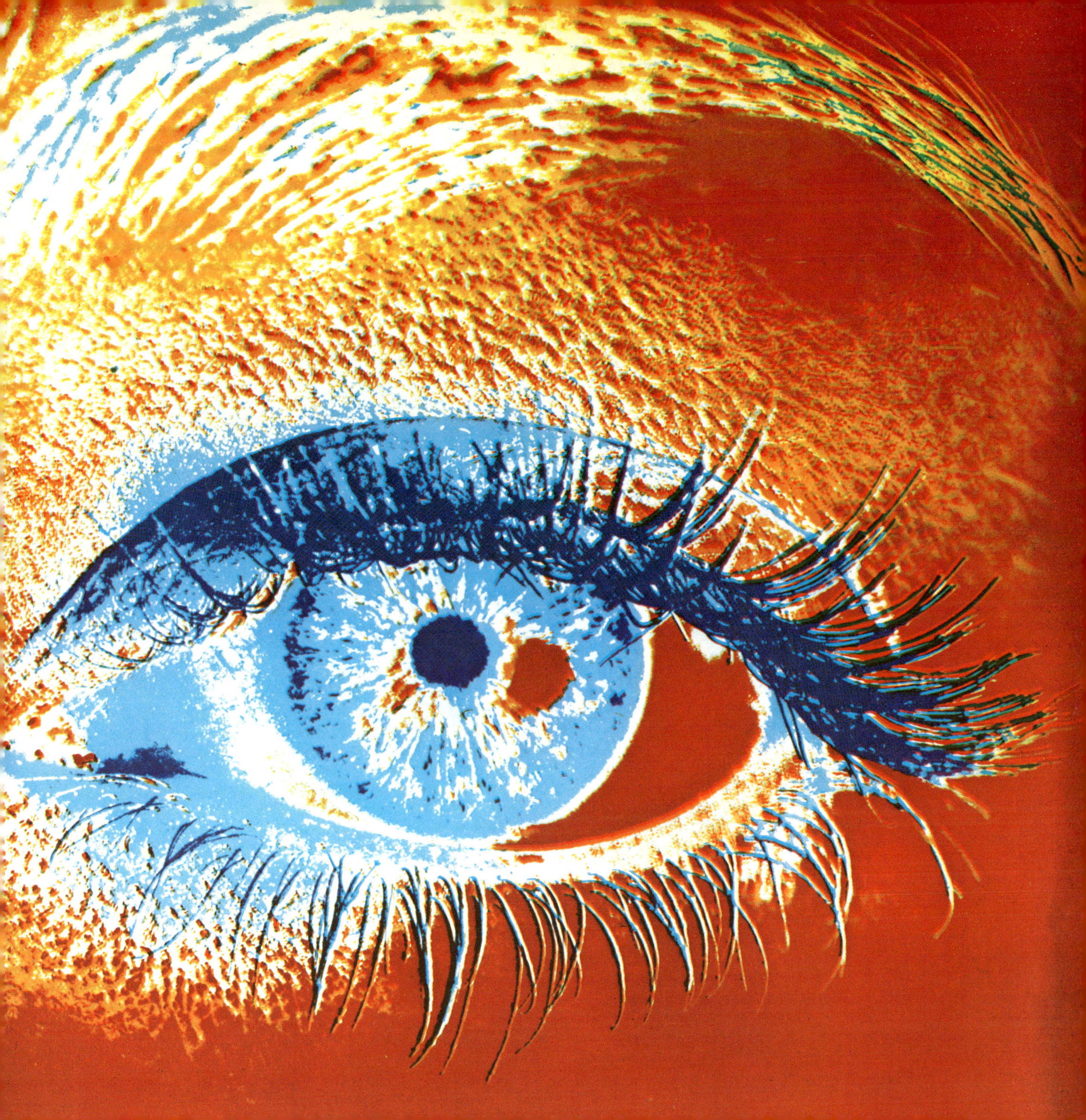

Color Solarization

Procedure

(1) Make an enlargement from a color slide onto color paper.

(2) Expose enlargement (after developing halfway) to colored light for about four seconds.

(3) Light source: 15 watt laboratory lamp with red filter; distance from enlargement, about two to three feet (60-80 cm).

.4) Continue the development process according to the manufacturer's recommendations.

Color solarization is realized by different technical processes. In principle, the color exposure is done during the first step in the color developer. This applies for solarization of color negatives, color transparencies, and even color enlarging papers. In all cases, the typical borderline between light and dark areas is formed.

In the image pictured, a paper enlargement was made from a color slide which was illuminated during development with red light. The unexposed image parts assumed the complementary color of the red-filtered light.

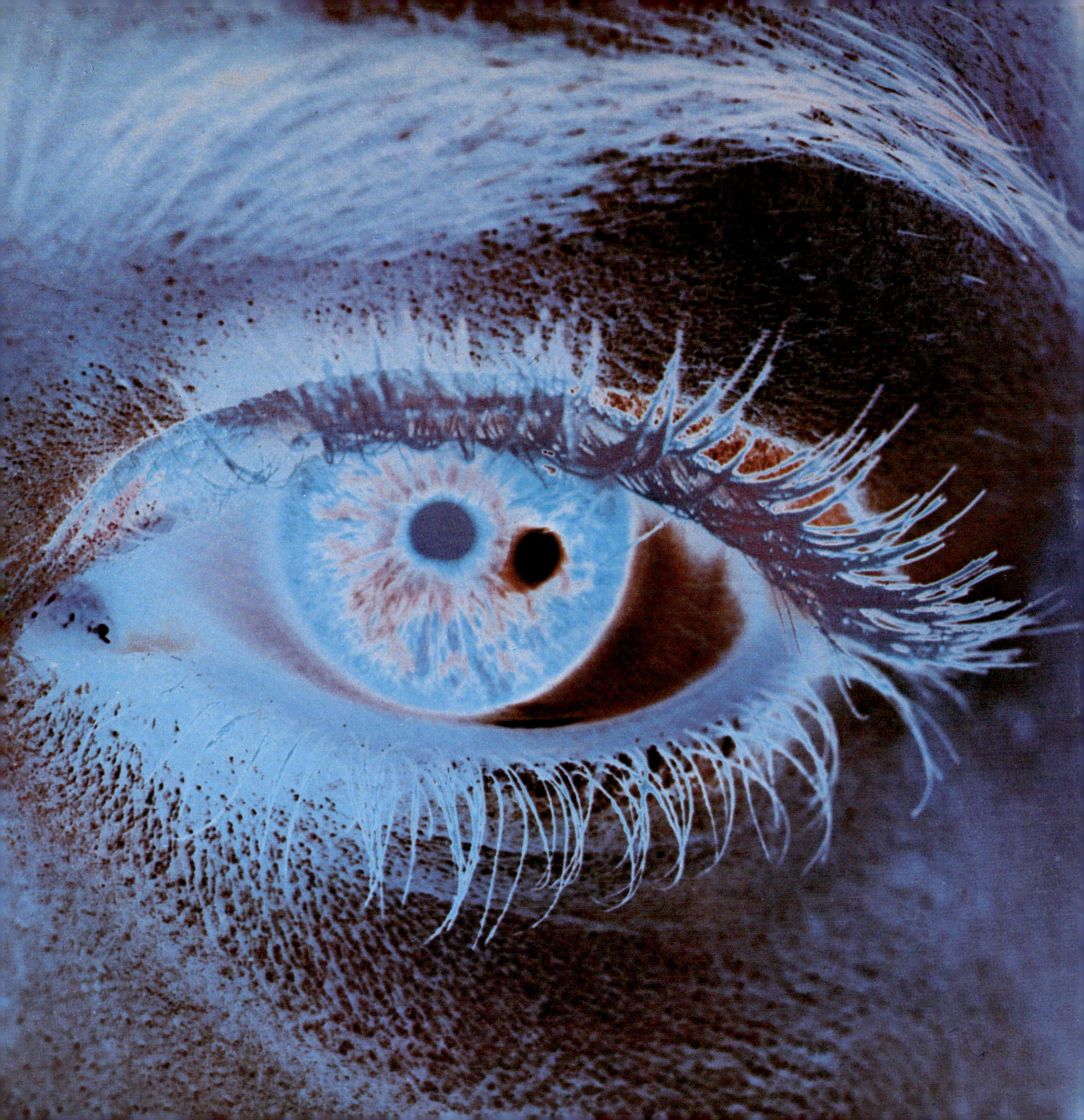

Color Solarization

Procedure

(1) See preceding page.
(2) Use green filter instead of the red one.

The adjacent example was processed as described on the preceding page. However, instead of a red filter, a green filter was used. The background hue changed in complementary colors to the filtration.

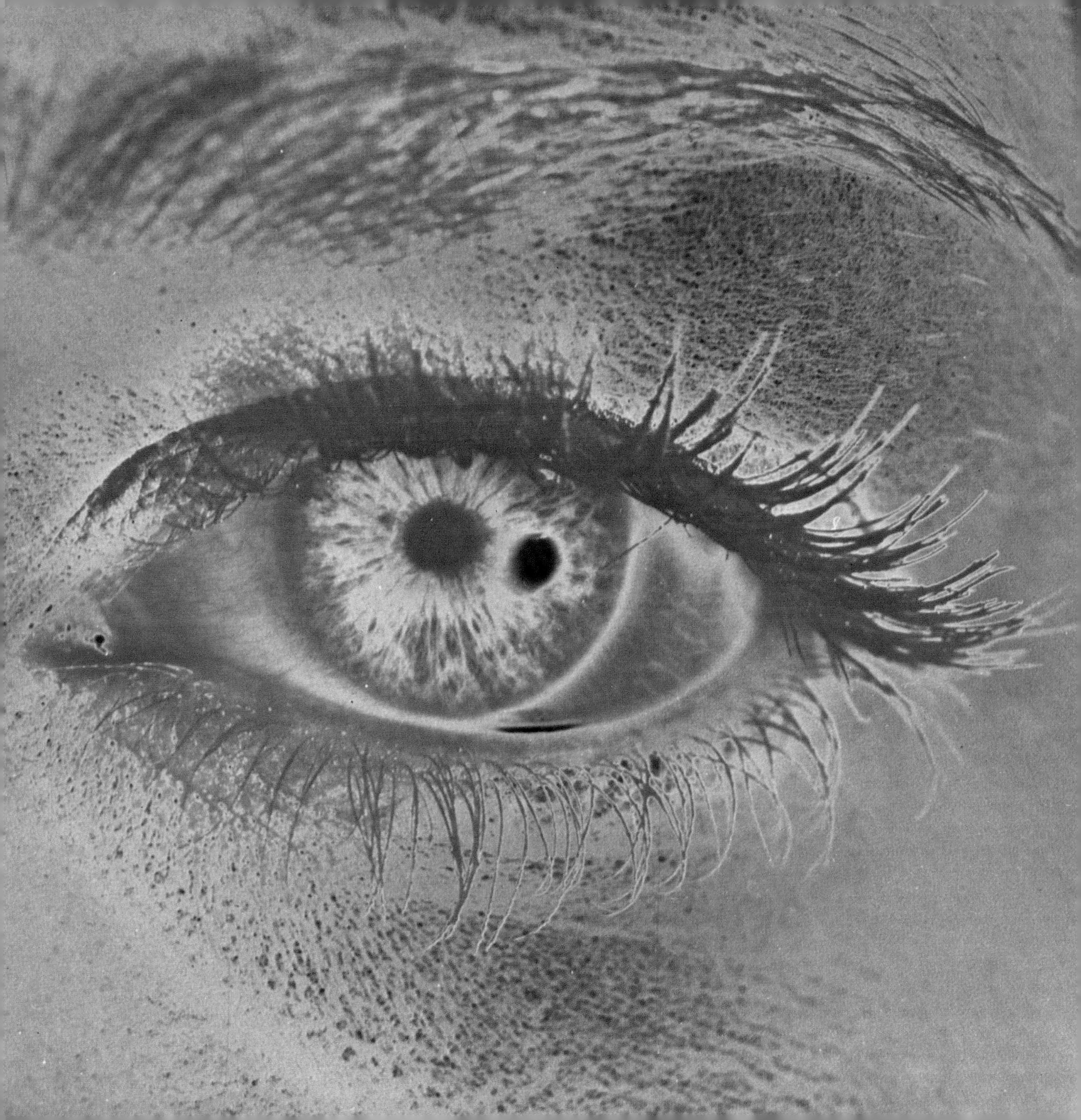

Color Solarization

An enhancement of the already shown color solarization is shown on the next page.

A color enlargement was made from a color slide solarized with red light. During the first development, the partially developed enlargement was again exposed to colored light.

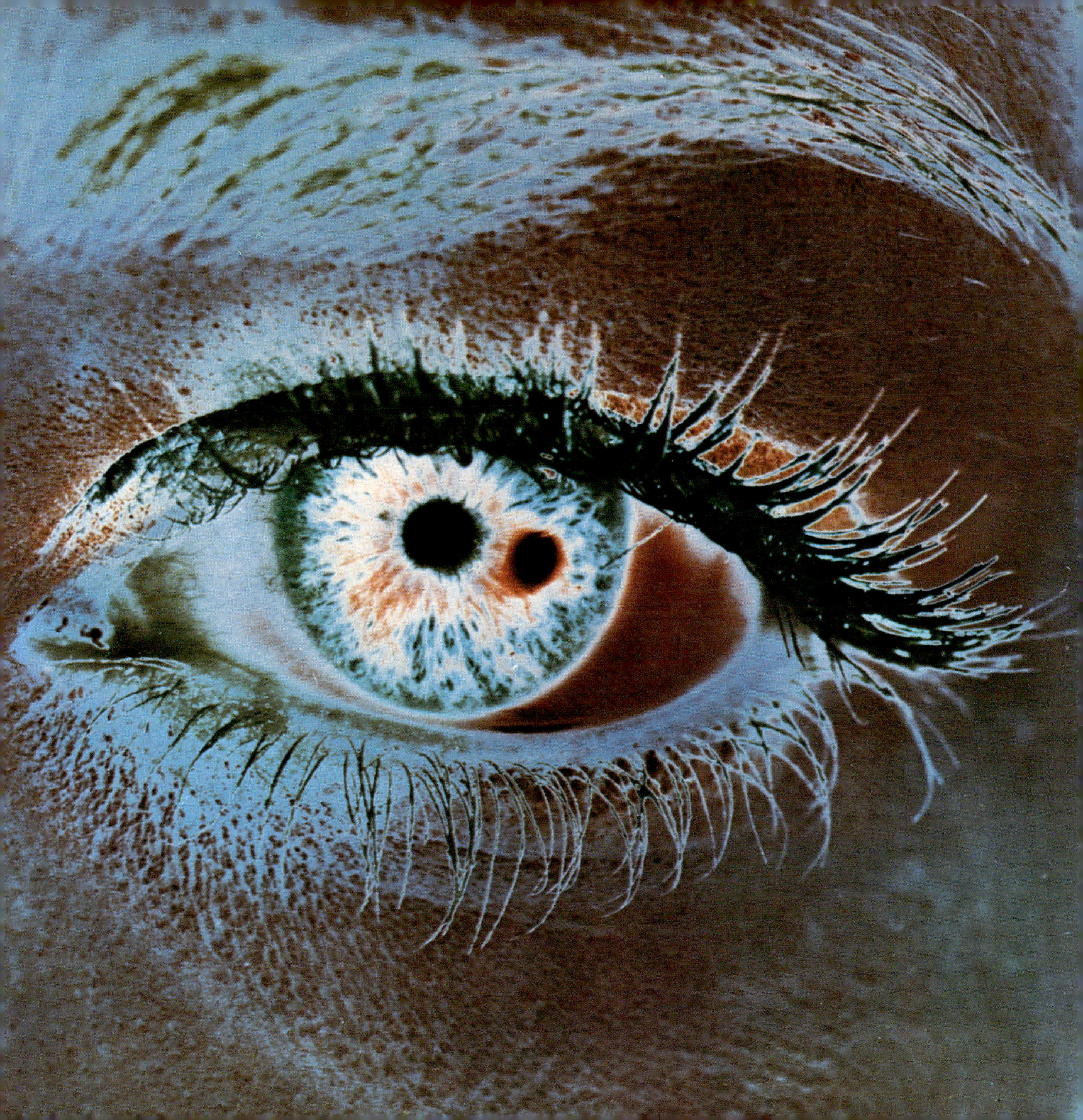

Agfacontour in Color

Procedure

(1) Camera aimed at illuminated image (1:1).
(2) Expose, while placing color filter before lens.
(3) Reproduce every further equidensity film in register together with the desired color.
(4) Process color slide film according to the manufacturer's recommendations.

On a multiple exposure, with a 6 × 6 reflex camera, several Agfacontour equidensity films are reproduced in register. The different forms are subsequently placed together with color filters in front of the camera lens and are exposed onto color slide film. A home-made illumination box is used.

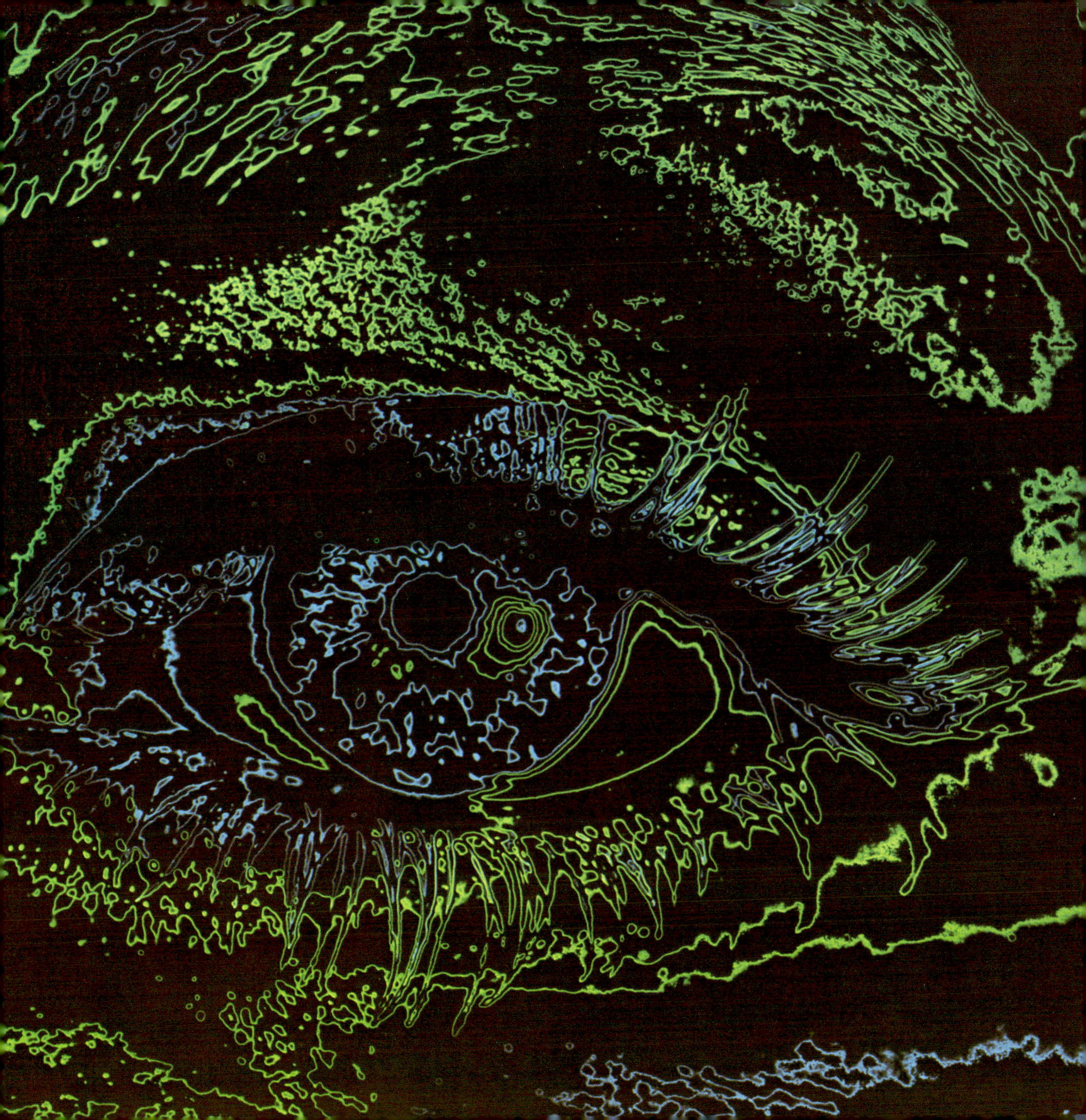

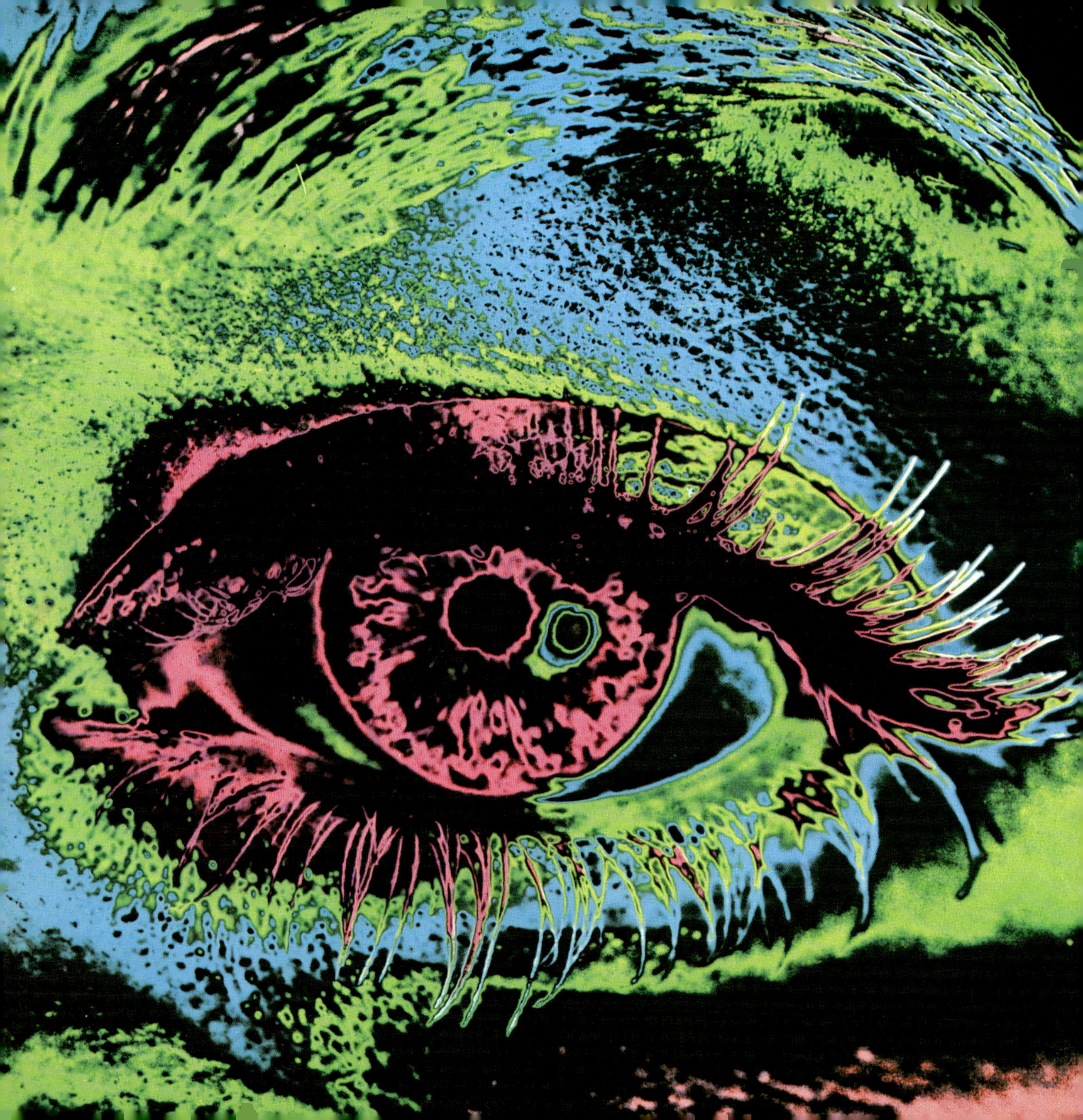

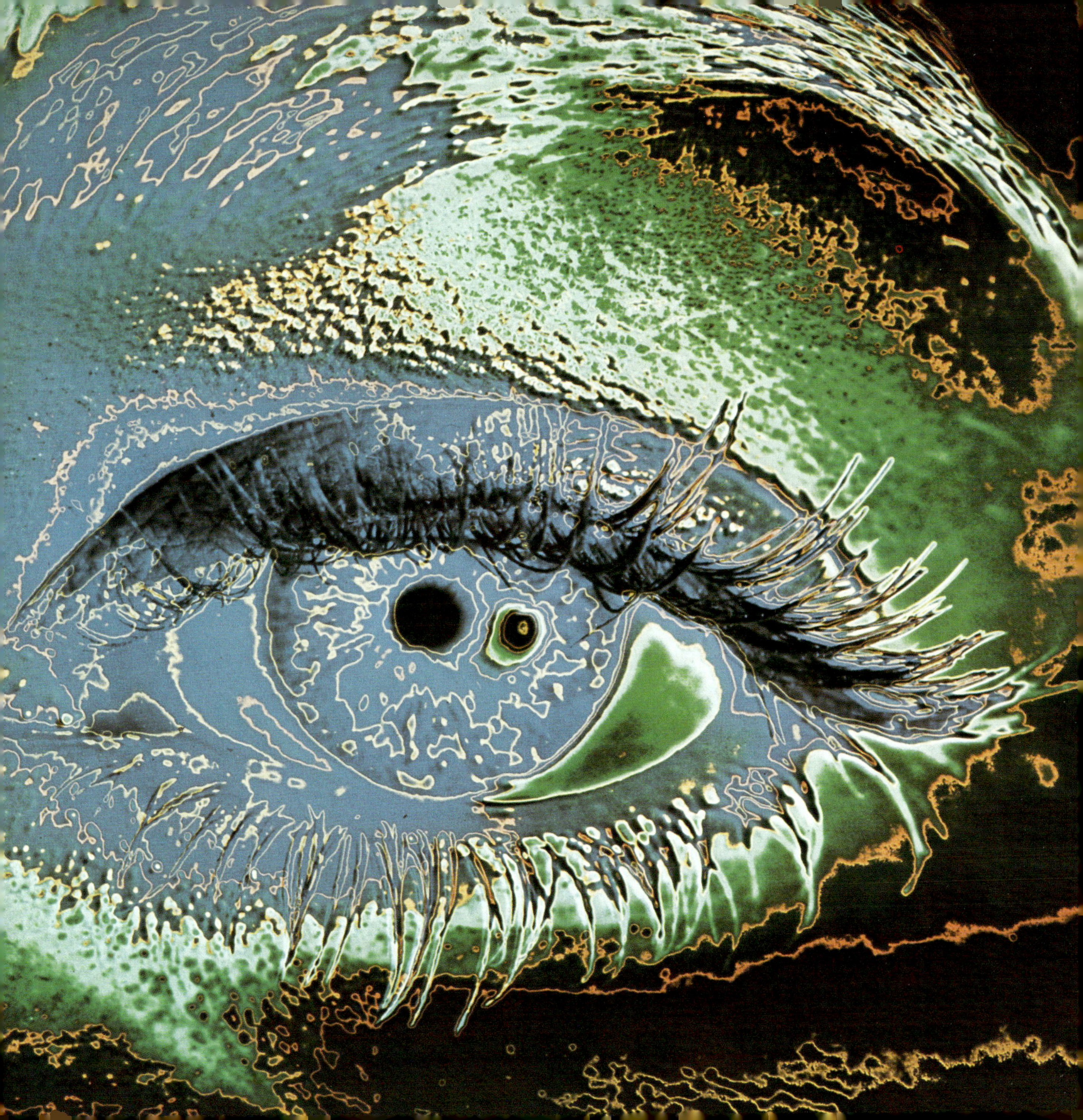

Color Relief

The effects of a color relief can be achieved with many different methods. Similar to a black-and-white relief, this effect appears by combining a color positive with a color negative. Since complementary colors of similar densities neutralize each other during superimposition, it is required to keep the color slide much less contrasty than the negative. Pure coloration in the result occurs when a positive black-and-white copied film of the same image is placed between the negative and the transparency which are copied onto color internegative film. This way, color is masked out on the black parts of the transparency. During exposure of this negative/positive superimposition, the pure color of the negative remains as the dominating color element.

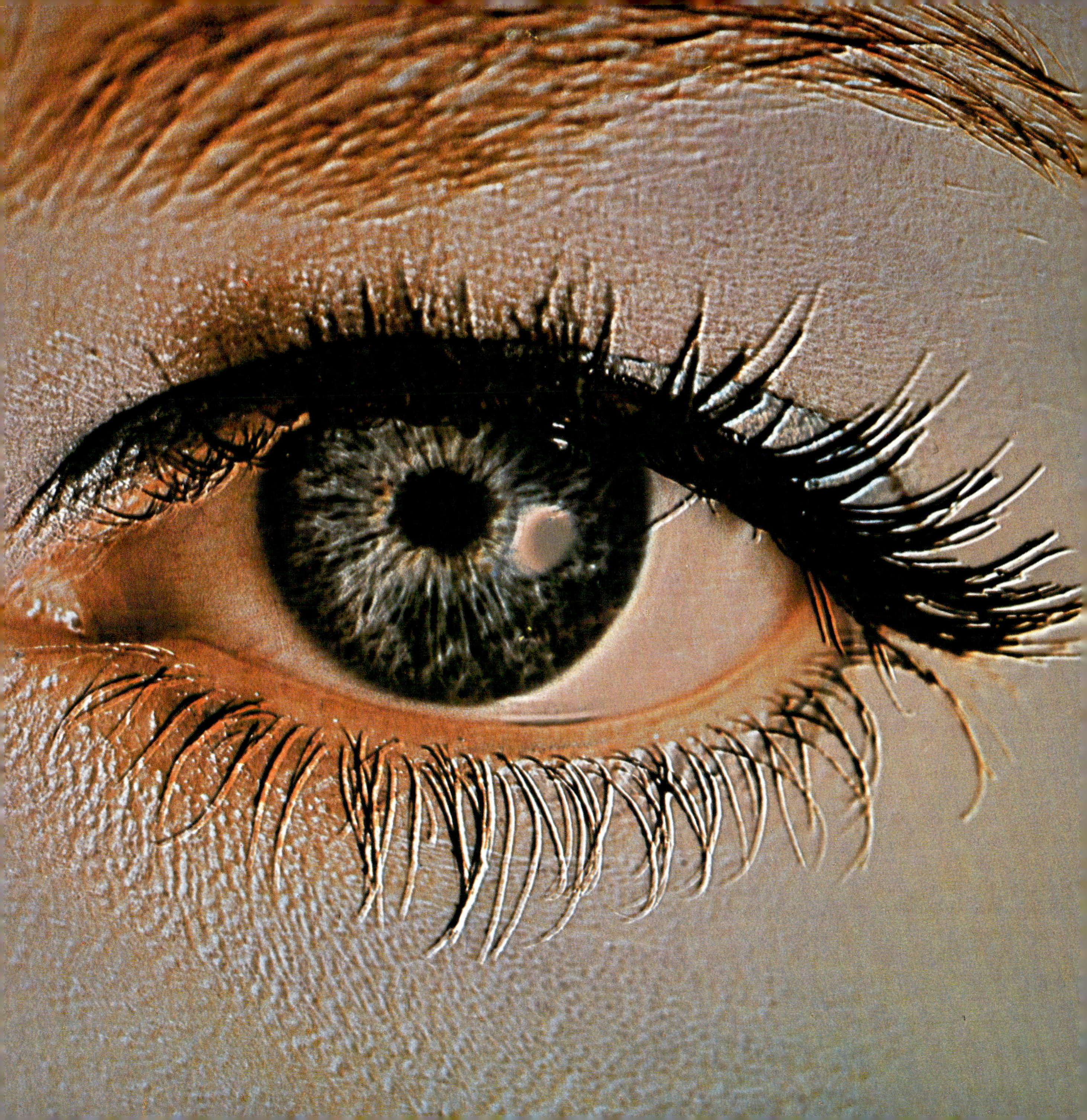

Color Relief

A further possibility to obtain relief effects is the combination of a color negative with a black-and-white line relief on film.

Procedure

(1) Put register markers on color negative.
(2) Make a positive from the color negative onto line film.
(3) Copy result into a negative.
(4) Mount positive and negative, right sides together, and recopy.
(5) (Result: linear positive relief.)
(6) Copy onto film to make a negative.
(7) Put color negative into enlarger and expose onto color paper.
(8) Re-expose negative from relief in same enlargement and in register on same color exposure.
(9) Follow the manufacturer's processing recommendations.

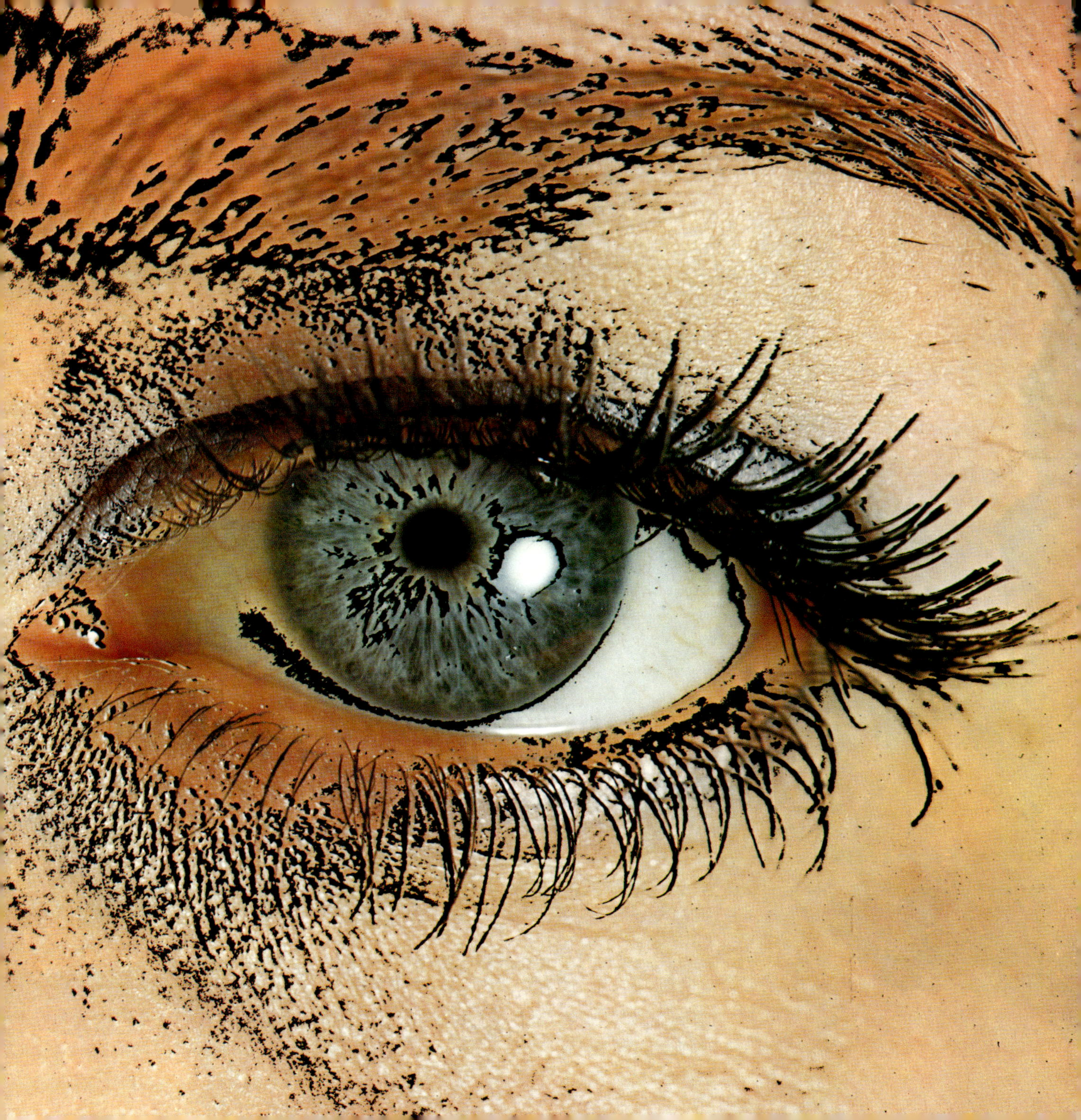

TYPOGRAPHY WITH PHOTOS

Typographic Modifications

<table>
<tr><td>

Procedure

(1) *Make a negative of the writing structure.*
(2) *Copy the film negative from the image, mount both negatives on top of each other.*
(3) *Expose onto extra-hard paper.*
(4) *Develop, stop, fix, wash, and dry.*

</td><td>

An interesting possibility is the combination of image and typography. A negative letter structure corresponding to the image on film is mounted with the negative copy of the original. After exposure, the form of the image remains as positive structure of the lettering.

</td></tr>
</table>

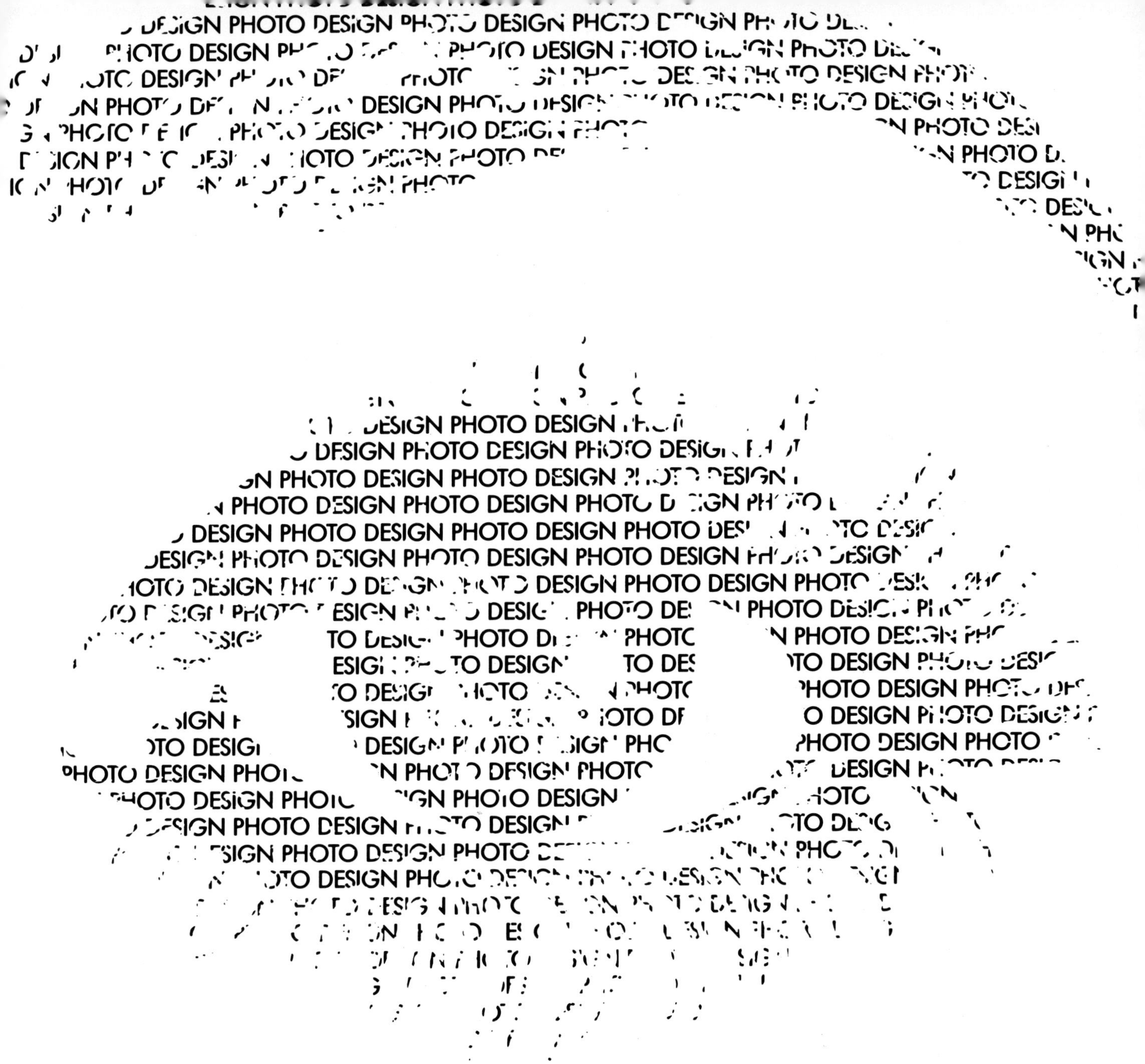

DESIGN PHOTO DESIGN PHOTO DESIGN PHOTO DESIGN PHOTO DE
PHOTO DESIGN PHOTO DESIGN PHOTO DESIGN PHOTO DES
PHOTO DESIGN PHOTO DESIGN PHOTO DESIGN PHOTO DESIGN PHOTO
PHOTO DESIGN PHOTO DESIGN PHOTO DESIGN PHOTO DESIGN PHOTO
PHOTO DESIGN PHOTO DESIGN PHOTO DESIGN PHOTO DESIGN
DESIGN PHOTO DESIGN PHOTO DESIGN PHOTO
HOTO DESIGN PHOTO DESIGN PHOTO
DESIGN PHOTO DESIGN PHOTO D.

DESIGN PHOTO DESIGN PHOTO
DESIGN PHOTO DESIGN PHOTO DESIGN PHOTO
GN PHOTO DESIGN PHOTO DESIGN PHOTO DESIGN
PHOTO DESIGN PHOTO DESIGN PHOTO DESIGN PHOTO
DESIGN PHOTO DESIGN PHOTO DESIGN PHOTO DESIGN PHOTO DESIGN
DESIGN PHOTO DESIGN PHOTO DESIGN PHOTO DESIGN PHOTO DESIGN
HOTO DESIGN PHOTO DESIGN PHOTO DESIGN PHOTO DESIGN PHOTO DESIGN PHOTO
TO DESIGN PHOTO DESIGN PHOTO DESIGN PHOTO DESIGN PHOTO DESIGN PHOTO
DESIGN TO DESIGN PHOTO DESIGN PHOTO DESIGN PHOTO DESIGN PHOTO
ESIGN PHOTO DESIGN TO DES TO DESIGN PHOTO DESIGN
TO DESIGN PHOTO PHOTO PHOTO DESIGN PHOTO DESIGN
DESIGN SIGN PHOTO DF O DESIGN PHOTO DESIGN
TO DESIGN DESIGN PHOTO DESIGN PHO PHOTO DESIGN PHOTO
PHOTO DESIGN PHOTO N PHOTO DESIGN PHOTO DESIGN PHOTO DESIGN
PHOTO DESIGN PHOTO GN PHOTO DESIGN DESIGN PHOTO
DESIGN PHOTO DESIGN PHOTO DESIGN DESIGN PHOTO DESIGN
DESIGN PHOTO DESIGN PHOTO DESIGN DESIGN PHOTO DESIGN
OTO DESIGN PHOTO DESIGN PHOTO DESIGN PHOTO DESIGN PHOTO DESIGN

Typographic Modifications

From the many possible image and letter structure combinations, here is another one. The result on the next page was obtained after mounting film with a positive lettering structure after positive copying of the image. After exposure onto extra-hard paper, the form of the motives appears negative in negative lettering on a black background.

Typographic Modifications

Lettering distorted with a fisheye lens is copied onto a solarized black-and-white enlargement. Lettering modifications in many variations are no problem for printing houses or laboratories. See the example on page 60 for modifications.

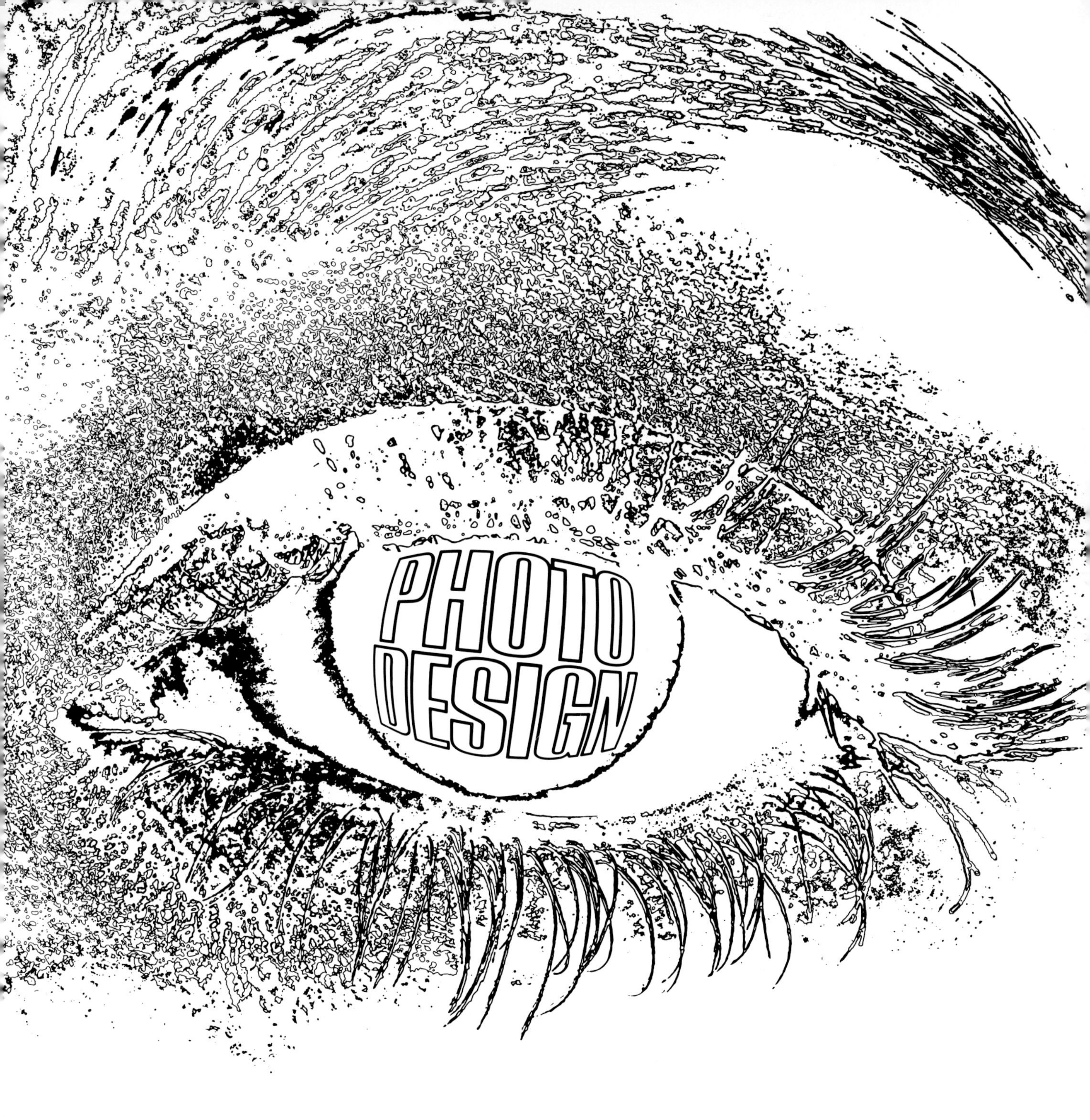

PHOTO
DESIGN

GRAPHIC VARIATIONS

Photo-Graphics

The finished enlargement can be changed graphically by cutting it apart. By moving, mixing, distorting, etc., the pieces, a multitude of different combinations are possible.

Page 127: Positive and negative enlargements separated on the middle vertical axis and mounted side by side.

Page 128: Positive and negative enlargements cut into strips in register, and then mounted alternately.

Page 129: Differently exposed continuous-tone enlargements cut in register into horizontal strips and mounted one under the other. Then cut vertically in squares and again mounted alternately in a checkerboard pattern.

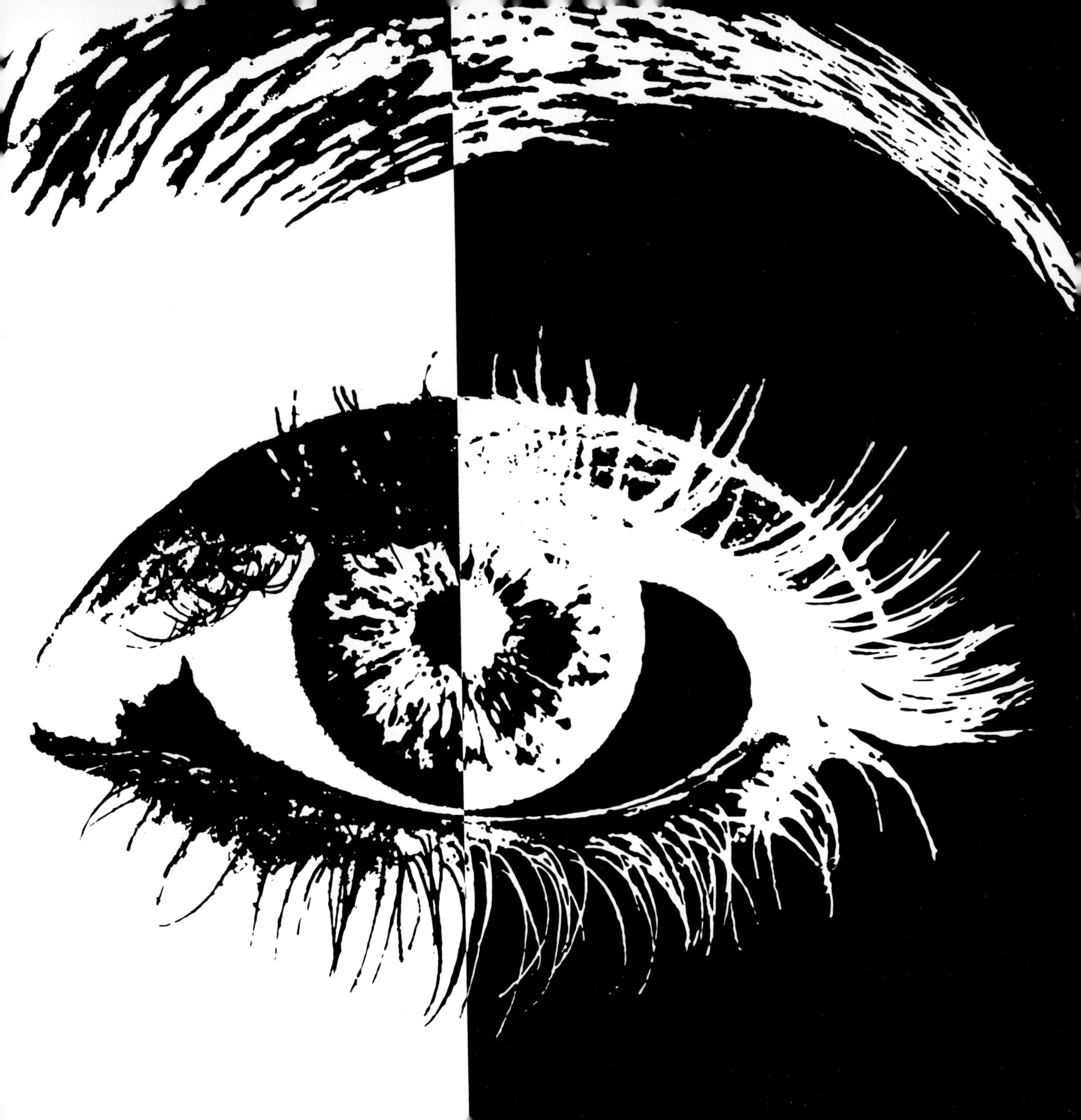

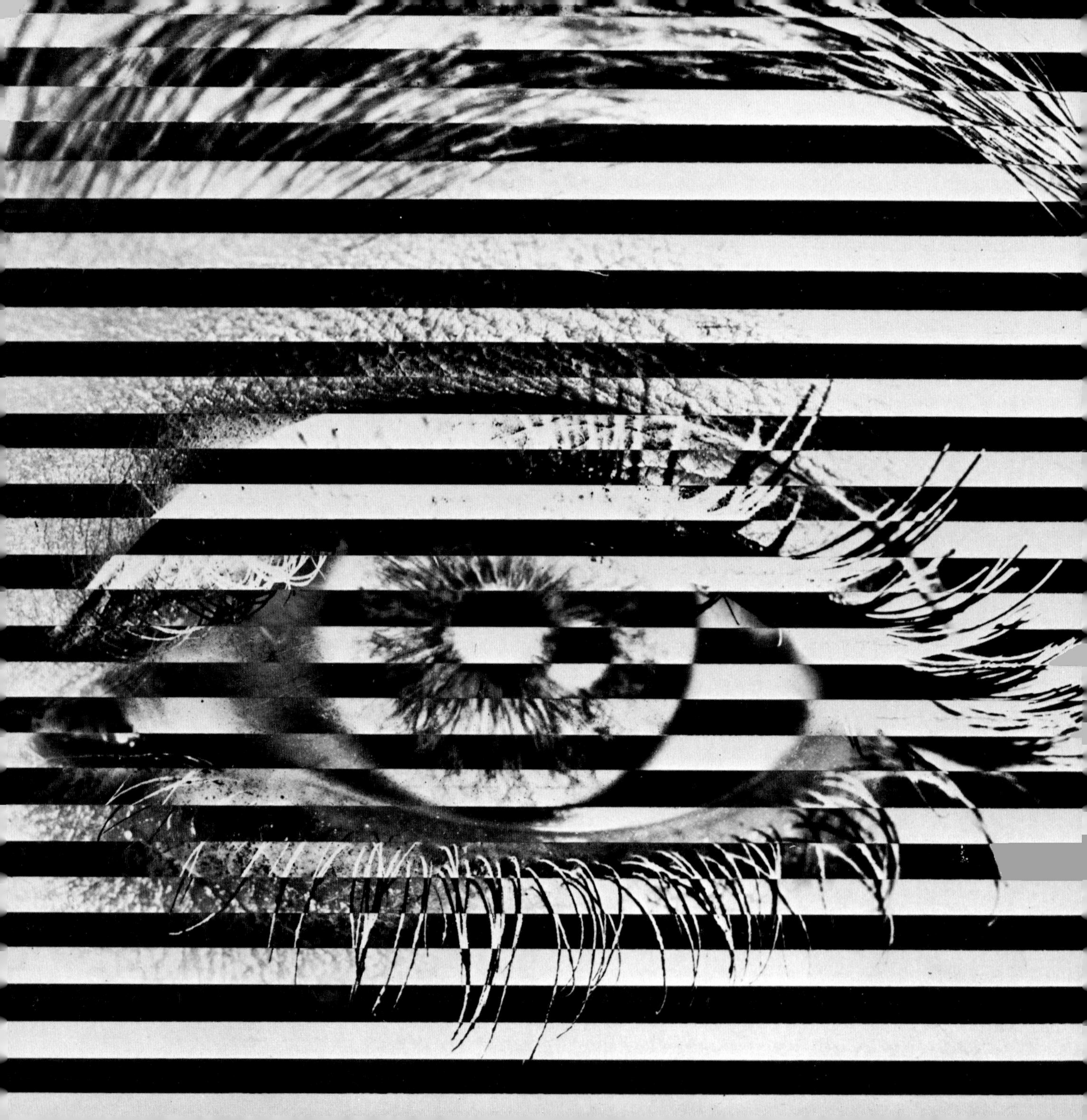

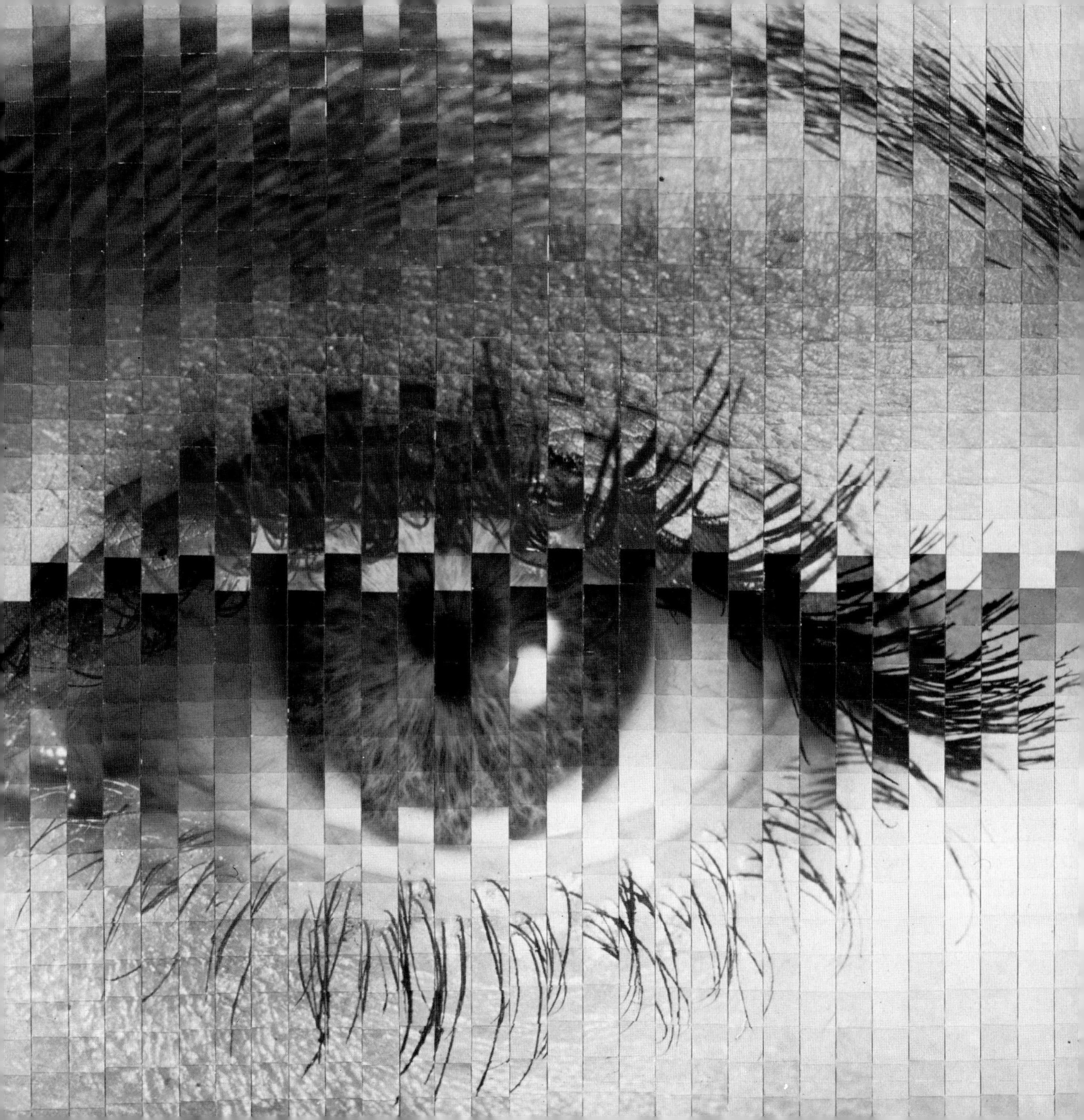

PRINTING

Coarse-Color Screen

An image can attain a strongly graphical character by using coarse-colored screening. From a printing house, one obtains a color screening set of four color separations, using a small format color negative or slide. The adjacent example was screened from a 2¼" × 2¼" (6 × 6 cm) color slide using a 25 line per inch (10 lines per cm) screen.

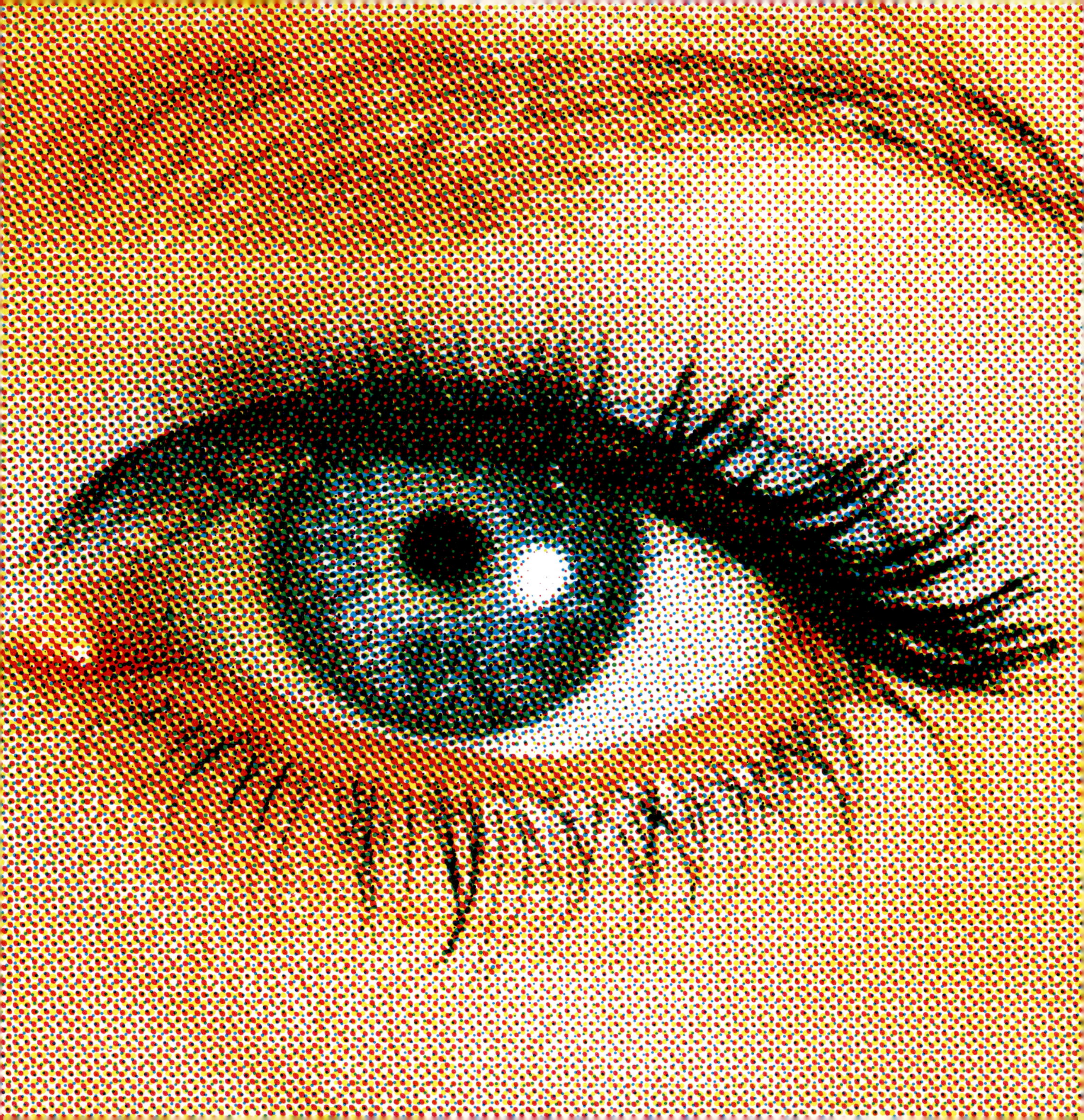

Fluorescent Colors

Fluorescent colors cause the invisible UV light to reflect and illuminate and are useful for many designs. With their intensity, these colors are strongly evident to the observer. The example on the right shows so-called iridescent contrast, achieved by using two complementary colors of equally bright hues.

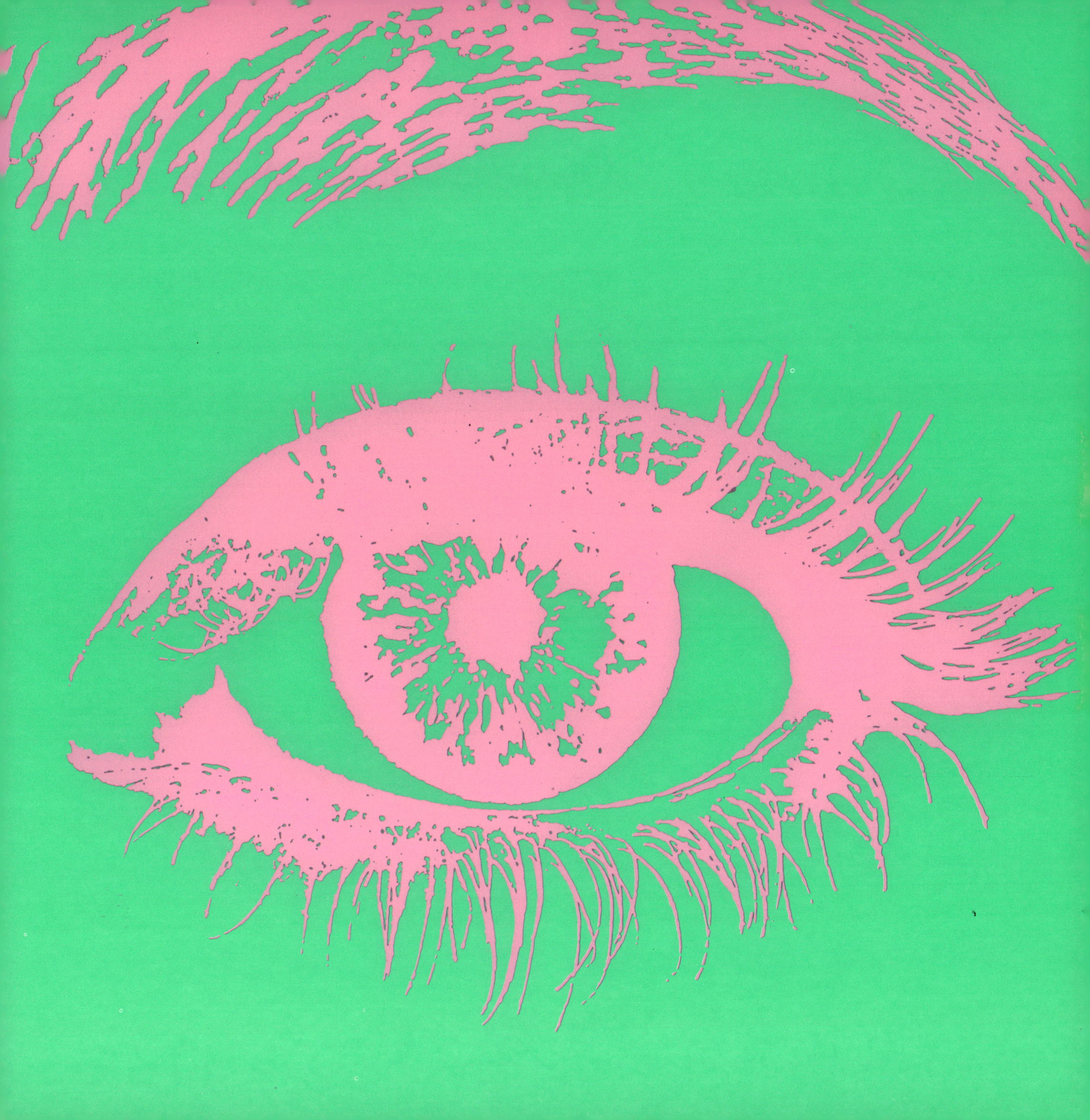

Fluorescent Colors

The fluorescent power of these colors is further intensified by using a black background. Such colors are highly aggressive and catch the attention. Therefore, they can be used for posters and other scenes which require attention, such as advertisements.

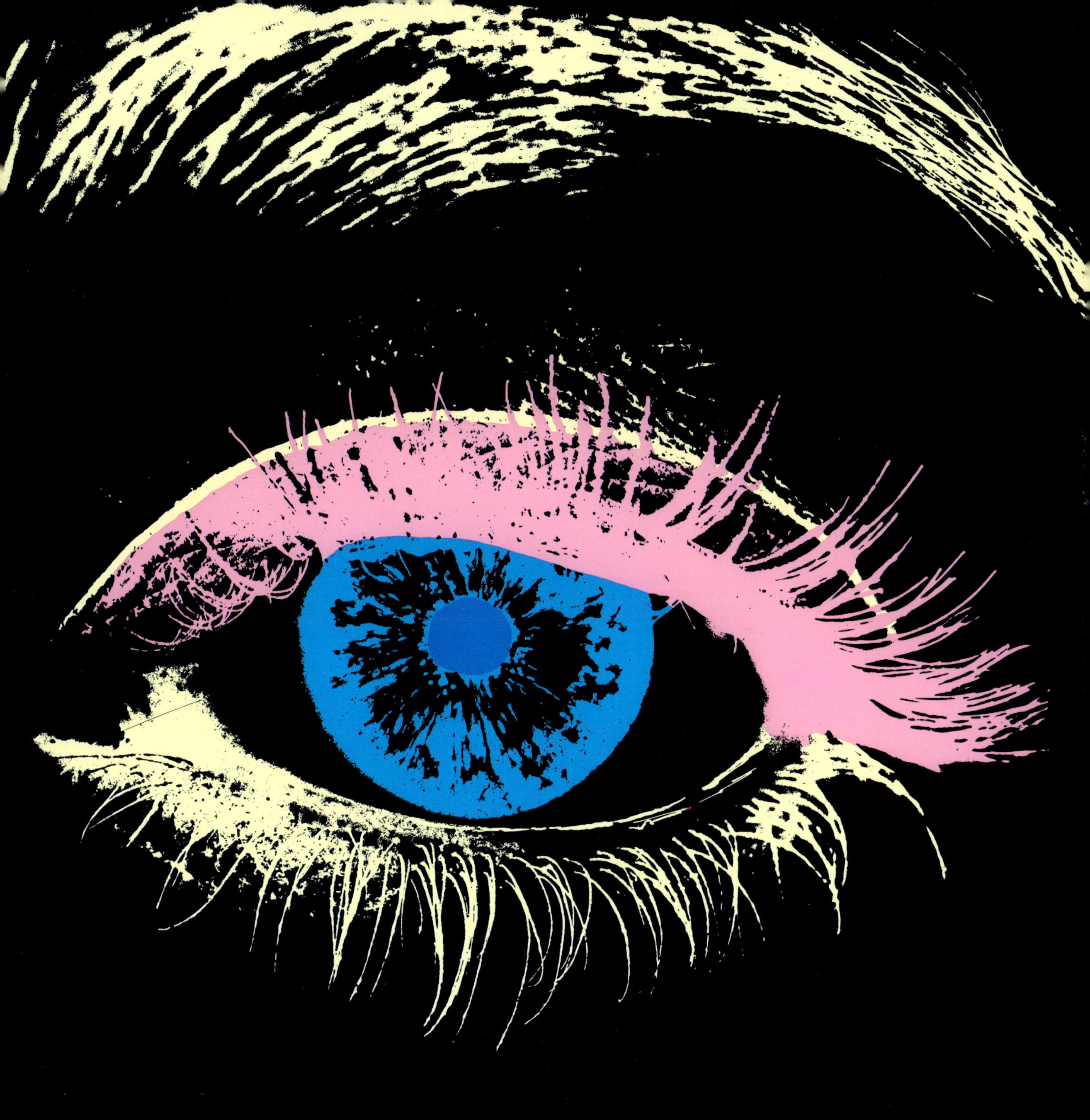

Metallic Colors

When printing with metallic colors, the object attains extraordinary characteristics. The metallic effects are obtained by mixing differently colored metal dust into the printing dyes. (For example, silver, copper, or gold dust.)

Hot Foil Stamping

A metallic reflecting form of a line motif printed on cardboard or paper is the essential characteristic of a hot foil stamping. By pressure and heat, one embosses a colored, high gloss adhesive foil onto the cardboard or paper during the printing process.

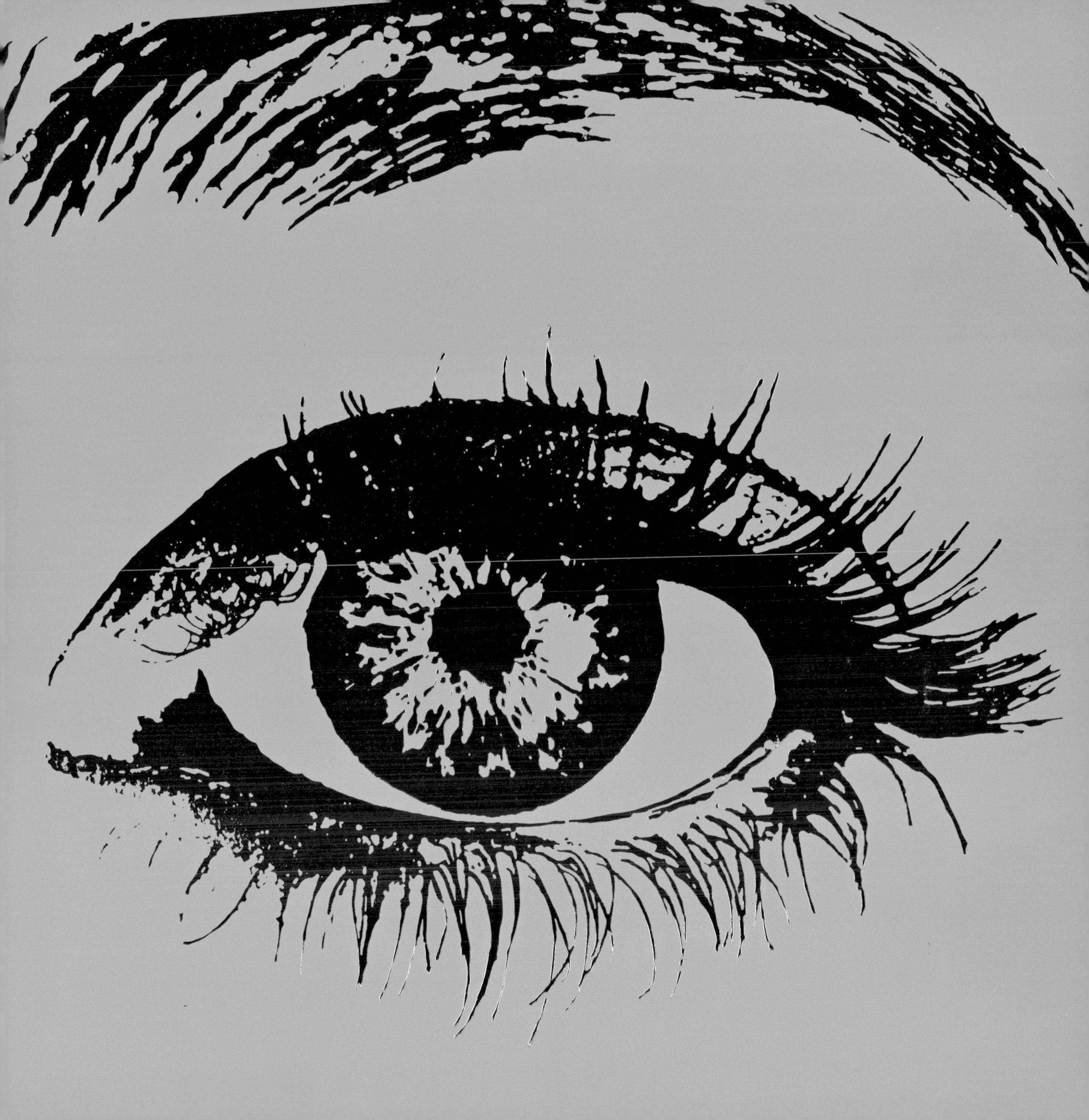

Embossing

Embossing, which is used mostly in letters or scriptures, can also render special effects to a photograph. The printer etches a stenciled printing plate from the line sample of the picture. The paper or cardboard is modified in the desired manner by moisture and pressure.